PENGUIN BOOKS

26/11 STORIES OF STRENGTH

The Indian Express is the flagship newspaper brand of the Express Group. From a single-edition paper in Madras in 1932, *The Indian Express* has grown into a multiple-edition paper influencing thought and policy across the country. Packed with news, knowledge and information, *The Indian Express* hits at the heart of the issue without any fear or favour. Read only by those who have their own unique points of view, its coverage is based on comprehensive analysis and fearless reporting. Its design is bold in its simplicity and evokes clarity and depth rather than noise and clutter, hence setting a benchmark for daily journalism's ability to inform and interpret, challenge and provoke. The group is also one of the world's largest digital news companies, with six languages, and clocking 150 million uniques per month around the world.

≋ The IndianEXPRESS

26/11

STORIES OF
STRENGTH

PRESENTED BY **facebook**

EDITED BY **KAVITHA IYER**

INTRODUCTION BY **ANANT GOENKA**

PENGUIN BOOKS

An imprint of Penguin Random House

PENGUIN BOOKS

USA | Canada | UK | Ireland | Australia
New Zealand | India | South Africa | China | Singapore

Penguin Books is part of the Penguin Random House group of companies
whose addresses can be found at global.penguinrandomhouse.com

Published by Penguin Random House India Pvt. Ltd
4th Floor, Capital Tower 1, MG Road,
Gurugram 122 002, Haryana, India

Penguin
Random House
India

First published in Penguin Books by Penguin Random House India 2018

ISBN 9780143446101

For sale in the Indian Subcontinent only

Typeset in Adobe Caslon Pro by Manipal Digital Systems, Manipal

Printed at Repro India Limited

www.penguin.co.in

MIX
Paper from
responsible sources
FSC® C047271

This is a legitimate digitally printed version of the book and therefore might not
have certain extra finishing on the cover.

*To the brave men and women of various agencies who
responded to the call of duty during the three-day siege of
Mumbai starting 26 November 2008*

*National Security Guard
Indian Army
Indian Navy, MARCOS
Indian Air Force
Indian Coast Guard
Mumbai Police
Intelligence Bureau
Research and Analysis Wing
Maharashtra Anti-terrorism Squad
Government Railway Police
Railway Police Force
Rapid Action Force
State Reserve Police Force
Mumbai Fire Brigade
Brihanmumbai Municipal Corporation*

Contents

Contents

Foreword

The Power of the Moderate

The Gateway of India, at first instance, appears to be an odd frame for the type of conversations that follow. It was, after all, built to commemorate a state visit of a foreign invader.

But rather than tearing down the Gateway after our liberation, we absorbed it and attached our own meanings—hospitable welcome and an openness to the world—to it while simultaneously leaving it intact as a reminder of the British Raj, so we knew that also passed. And it passed because of our collective might. We overcame it by the solidarity of peaceful resistance.

The Gateway, therefore, in its contemporary complexity of meanings, is a locus of reflection and debate. There could not be a more appropriate symbol to commemorate the cowardly attacks on 26 November 2008 at various places across our city.

To me, these attacks were a wake-up call. But the question I asked myself was: 'Wake up, yes, but wake up to what?'

I woke up to a new era of violence, a new kind of violence—one inflicted by terrorism. I woke up to the fact that terrorism is not an ideology. It is an act of scaring a peaceful people; an act of evoking the fear of sudden, untimely death. It is an act of negotiating at gunpoint.

Terrorism is not an act of faith. Terrorism can never replace another ideology. Whatever the political rhetoric may be, terrorism is neither a form of justice nor an instrument of justice. It is the whimsical randomness of evil.

So how does an unarmed, peaceful humanity fight the fear of terrorism's sudden violence? How does anyone who believes in a life of merit and hard work begin to believe in the authority of guns and bombs? Will armed mercenaries decide the future of our children? Will the threat of violence point us to the causes that we fight for? Will terror decide what is true–false, correct–incorrect, good–bad and right or wrong?

No.

Terror does no such thing; terror does not decide anything. Terror only hopes to bluff that evil can be stronger than humanity, that hate can be mightier than love. It is now for each one of us to decide if we want our children to accept this evil doctrine or show them that terror does not have a place in our hearts.

An estimated 20-lakh people were killed during the Partition of our country in 1947, and several times more displaced. When people are divided by distrust, when friends and neighbours stop trusting each other, when a nation turns into hostile islands of fear, then our world is broken into fragments, divided by narrow domestic walls. This is precisely what terror aims to achieve.

Terror does not preserve anything, it is designed to destroy. Once unleashed, terror cannot be stopped by a debate. An act of terror, therefore, is not open to negotiations or to wisdom. It can only be repelled, repulsed and destroyed by a more powerful reaction. There are no two ways about that. A corrective action is necessary.

But it does not end there. When a farm is infested by weeds, a weed-killer does not stop them from growing again after the next rains. The farmer has to pull them out, one by one, every single weed, by its roots.

Terror must be rooted out. We know that the war on terror worldwide has not eliminated the root cause of terrorism so far. And it doesn't look likely, if the same method is expected to generate different results.

And here is where I think we must fall back on Mahatma Gandhi's satyagraha, which in its truest form is the persuasion of truth.

The perception that moderates are not relevant in the war on terror is rather myopic. Moderates are not part of this struggle because both the handlers of terror and the agents of resistance consider them to be passive and disempowered. Yet, the prime victims of terror are the moderates. More than 70 per cent of our nation is moderate. And as moderates, we must recognize that to vilify a foe is no victory at all, but to understand a foe is the first act of strength in resistance.

And to understand a foe, one must first understand oneself. To understand ourselves, we must ask not what we are against, for that is defining ourselves by the ideas of our foe, by their power. Rather, to understand ourselves, we must ask what we are for. We can only understand ourselves together.

To understand ourselves as a collective is to find the time for debate, discussion, argument, listening to each other, trying to understand differing points of view, engaging, challenging our ways of thinking and honouring each other with compassion. These are the answers to violence and death. If we are to be for anything, then to start with, what we must be for is each other. That is solidarity, and history has shown that our country's solidarity is as strong as an oak tree.

The colonial rulers laughed at Mahatma Gandhi when he spoke of this vision. His passive resistance suffered unimaginable brutality during its campaign. But we know the result—it demolished the foundations of imperialism from the face of the earth.

The time has come for us moderates to unite once again. It is time to invoke the Mahatma's satyagraha of peaceful, non-violent non-cooperation. We must boycott not only violence, but also everything that breeds it. We must rise up in one voice as a nation of moderates, and say:

'No!'

To the terrorist that one 'no' will have the most impact. It's very simple: a parasite cannot kill and survive in the same host at the same time. We must refuse to host terrorists. And today standing at the foot of the Gateway, this is my prayer:

'All those who live for humanity, all those who live for the children of tomorrow, must now realize that it is time to rise, and say, "No!" Uproot every weed from your surroundings. Do not threaten, do not fight, do not kill, do not injure. Simply refuse to cooperate, at any cost.

Do not feed the evil; do not host the parasite called the terrorist. And then, may we all live in the dream of Gurudev's words: 'Into that Heaven of Freedom, my Father, let my country awake.'

Amitabh Bachchan
Mumbai 2018

Introduction

The first comment one hears while discussing India with anyone is just how young our population is. We are 800 million Indians under the age of thirty-five. And for most of us in this 800-million-strong cohort, two events have shaped the way we think about terrorism and organized violence—the 2001 attack on the Parliament, and the three-day siege of Mumbai in November 2008. And with every attack, wherever in the world it might be and whatever its scale, the 800 million of us, who were at our most impressionable age ten years ago, are reminded of the rage and despair we felt on 26 November 2008.

Across the world, the media has captured these tragedies as trauma and statistic, dwelling on the anger and insecurity around the event. If economic progress led us to bury our fear and hate in a dark corner of our hearts, news coverage of such events, amplified by social media, serves to effervesce those emotions.

News broadcasts, in a bid to make great prime time TV, rile up viewers. They rouse our anger at the neighbour's sheer hatred for our country, or our pride in its valiant armed forces. Admittedly, there may be something to gain from a little patriotism directed towards millennials who haven't had much exposure to stories of India's freedom struggle and who are increasingly uninterested in the idea of India. But as the media, for how long can we continue to assume that news consumers are incapable of discernment?

At *The Indian Express*, therefore, we decided that we must give more space in our pages to those who lived with the attacks as part of their individual family histories. It's important to hear how they processed these events ten years later; what course their lives took after the event.

These are incredibly inspiring stories of overcoming pain and bitterness, of courage. Surprisingly, the survivors' faith in humanity seemed stronger than the spectators'. This is what inspired this book.

Extremism stems in the mind. Too much of our intellectual bandwidth—column centimetres in newspapers, airtime on news channels and screen time on WhatsApp—is spent on finding people to be angry at, to hate and to blame. We tend to forget that we are all part of the problems we complain about—global warming, floods, and most importantly, the incessant fear and hate mongering that we don't do our parts to curb.

A terrorist attack anywhere in the world triggers in us all sorts of extremist ideas and views. Just remember the conversations you had or heard in the privacy of your homes after the attacks in Paris, Brussels and London. Remember just how vulnerable and frustrated you felt afterwards. And how, very often, you have been encouraged to think of someone—law enforcement agencies or the political leadership of another country or even historical figures—as the root cause of the incidents. Every terror strike, sparks an internal dialogue between the humanist and the extremist in us. And it is easy for the extremist to win, because when innocents die, extreme thoughts are easily rationalized.

And extremism leads us to take comfort in what we identify as ours; unites us with people based on our insecurities instead of our strengths. Then the justifications for our combined insecurities and fears render impossible any attempt to empathetically and constructively engage with the 'other' people.

Extremism, as David Brooks said so eloquently in the *New York Times*, 'makes you stupider. Instead of cleverly working to advance your own interest in a changing context, you end up shouting your own moral justifications into a whirlwind. Instead of restating your own values— for pluralism, for a compromise, for peace—you end up another soiled part of the climate.'[1]

And yet, many of the over sixty-five families that our teams in Mumbai interviewed over two years have emerged as humanists instead of extremists. And our interest lies in understanding how this happened. Kia Scherr who lost

---

[1] David Brooks, 'The Gaza Violence: How Extremism Corrupts', *New York Times*, 17 May 2018.

her daughter and husband in the attacks spoke of forgiving their murderers. Twenty-one-year-old Aditya Sharma said with candour that if he held on to the loss of his father, he'd be unable to come out of the cycle of negativity initiated by the killers. At nineteen, Shilpa Shaikh put her own life on hold to raise her dead sister's two little boys.

Of course, not all conversations are about moving on. One teenager has slowly but surely been lured towards Islamophobia. So what makes one child decide to open a charity for children of all communities while another paints an entire community with a bloody brush?

The book also provides an insight into raising a national hero. Our conversation with Major Sandeep Unnikrishnan's parents shows that he was destined to be a hero. At a young age, he convinced his mother to let go of her family inheritance simply because they didn't need it; he wanted them to give as generously as they could. Our reporter Mayura Janwalkar takes you to Tukaram Omble's hometown, a village of 250-odd houses separated by paddy fields, about 300 km from Mumbai. Here we see how passionately people have preserved the legacy of a committed policeman who, even ten years after his death, is remembered fondly for the simplicity, love and sense of duty he had always displayed. Just eight years old at the time of the attacks, Devika Rotawan developed the courage to depose in court as an eyewitness, having been shot in the leg at Chhatrapati Shivaji Terminus on that fateful night.

These are conversations that must become part of our news cycle. As mediapersons, we have a responsibility to encourage our readers to think beyond assigning blame. In hearing from those who were left behind after 26/11, we see just how humane some of their ideas are.

To what degree does Indianness have to do with how these individuals have dealt with their losses? After all, as a people, hardships aren't alien to us anywhere in the country. Is it in our DNA to respond to problems in a better way?

In a extensively researched piece, Harvard Professor Rohit Deshpande said he couldn't understand what made the Taj employees go beyond their call of duty and put their lives at stake to rescue guests that night. He studied the phenomenon and concluded that the reason the Taj employees acted so differently was because of Taj's hiring policies. He says that the hospitality division of the Tata Group of companies prefers hiring and training people from smaller cities. They choose to hire youngsters who have lived with their grandparents and are deeply respectful of the elders in their families.

One thing we know about India is that we're a country that has for hundreds of years been highly spiritual and god-fearing. But an increasing cohort of millennials, highly educated and aspiring professionals, look at events such as 26/11 and feel disenchanted by religion. Given that terror attacks are often connected with religion, if a millennial rolls her eye on the subject, it leaves the battleground open to the ones who care the most about it—extremists.

And so, today, more than ever before, I find that the educated moderate must have a view on religion, and must play an important balancing role against extremism.

Religions across the world, and more so in India, are not going away anywhere and will only become more important parts of our identities henceforth. In fact, according to Rabbi Jonathan Sacks, the world in the twenty-first century will be more religious than it was in the twentieth century. Even in China, a country that Chairman Mao declared as religion-free, there are more people who attend a place of worship once a week than members of the Communist Party.

And this is surprising, because as Sacks says in a conversation with Professor Charles Taylor, today we don't need revelation or magic or the Book of Psalms; we have science, technology and modern medicine. So in functional terms, everything religion used to do is now done by something else. And yet, people believe. Because neither science nor technology or free markets can answer the three fundamental questions of human beings, as Sacks defines them—'Who am I?' 'Why am I here?' 'How then shall I live?'

So religion, however we choose to see it, is at the centre of our lives as meaning–seeking beings. And nowhere has faith played a bigger role in humanism than in India.

Consider the story of Maulana Imdadul Rashidi from Asansol in West Bengal—a state that has been plagued by an alarming number of communal incidents over the past few years. Maulana Rashidi lost his son in one such communal incident. *The Indian Express* was there when many went to the grieving father, promising retaliation. Even in his grief, the maulana declared: 'If there is any retaliation, I will leave this area and no longer be associated with you.'

We would consider our endeavour successful if, upon reading these accounts, you are encouraged to think of what

Indianness is, and what you would like Indianness to be. Can we attempt to respond to the question Mr Bachchan has raised in the foreword—that we must define ourselves by what we are for and not by what we are against? Can something powerful be reintroduced as an idea of what an Indian should be like? Of how we would like to raise our children? We may learn something, perhaps, from the fact that those closest to Major Unnikrishnan and API Omble weren't at all surprised that these two acted heroically. These individuals stood out in their communities. Can we learn from them when we think of what kind of Indians we want to raise?

Because we cannot and, in my view, should not take religion out of India. Instead, we should find ways to shape our expectations around it. It's up to each one of us to find the gifts in ancient texts and philosophies, rather than challenging and judging them on the basis of the most destructive interpretations available.

Our 'Stories of Strength' project has, over the past three years, spent time with over sixty-five families impacted by 26/11. We are immensely grateful to all of them who have graciously and generously picked up the pieces of their hearts that were shattered ten years ago and shared with us their most vulnerable and personal moments. And in equal strength, we are grateful to those who did not—your stories motivate us to continue our project knowing that so much remains unfinished.

We understand the enormous responsibility we have when we point a camera at them and ask them to share these stories. We recognize that we may be forcing out extremely uncomfortable memories.

But we ask because we think it's important. It's important to speak—their voice should be a mirror to society. Not just because it's the tenth anniversary of the attacks, but because it's the 150th birth anniversary of the man whose methods, as Mr Bachchan says, ultimately defeated the foreign invader.

Because somewhere between revenge and forgiveness lies our reality. And the path we must walk on between these two extremes has to be led by those who were left behind after the attacks.

Because it is their ability to overcome fear that defines ours, their ability to channelize anger and inspire courage that inspires ours. It is their feeling of unity with each and every one of us that decides the unity of our society. And most of all, it is their undying faith in humanity that renews ours.

Sirf aap humein dikha sakte hain badla aur maafi ke beech ka rasta.

Aap hi humein batayenge sabhya samajh ki taakat.

Because if a few foolish, misguided cowards think they can decide how we die, they must know that they cannot decide how we live.

Anant Goenka
Executive Director
Indian Express Group

Chittaprosad, *Untitled*, linocut, mid-twentieth century
Collection: DAG

1

Ten Years of Grief and Pride

Kavitha Iyer

When a news channel first identified the major killed at the Taj Mahal Palace and Tower Hotel in Mumbai, Dhanalakshmi Unnikrishnan was cooking in the kitchen of their home in Yelahanka, Bangalore. It was mid-morning on Friday, 28 November. The television was on, but she wasn't paying attention. They had spoken to their son, Major Sandeep Unnikrishnan, on the night of 26, not long after Maharashtra's top antiterror policeman had been declared dead in what appeared, even as early as the first night of the siege, to be one of the worst-ever terrorist attacks in the country. Sandeep had spoken to them from the National Security Guard (NSG) hub in Manesar, Haryana, the home base of the elite commando unit.

A stickler for rules surrounding sensitive operations, Sandeep had not mentioned that he would be leaving for Mumbai. He'd told his father, K. Unnikrishnan, that Maharashtra ATS chief Hemant Karkare had been killed. And so, the television remained on through 27 November. 'We watched the news, and prayed for the operation to end soon, successfully,' Dhanalakshmi says. There would be time to discuss it at length later, for Sandeep was to come home on holiday in mid-December. And this time he was going to teach her to ride, first a bicycle and then a scooter.

But when a news channel's ticker flashed the slain officer's name, Unnikrishnan was watching the television alone. Minutes later, the news was confirmed. 'He came up behind me and put his hand on my shoulders. It felt as if his hand had no strength left in it; it just fell,' the sixty-six-year-old remembers.

He broke the news to her as gently as he could, his voice trembling, and she pounded him on the chest with both palms, furious. 'I was screaming. How could he say such a thing about his son,' she recounts. Then, food still on the stove, she ran out of the house, barefoot. She ran to the very end of their street, about 200 metres, before collapsing.

'I wasn't unconscious, not even for a second. In fact I couldn't have been more conscious. My mind raced back, back and back.' Almost presciently, Sandeep had joked with her on multiple occasions about dying young.

'Once he'd told me there would be many boys and girls to look after me if he died.' But her flashback took her farther that day, to every moment when she'd known that Sandeep was special in a way few others are. He was incredibly helpful, even as a child he was ready to take the rap for others. As a teenager, he was an unusually good leader, a pathfinder and problem-solver. It seemed almost logical that he'd died a hero.

Less than two months later, Dhanalakshmi accepted Sandeep's Ashok Chakra, the country's highest peacetime gallantry award. The citation reads:

Major Sandeep Unnikrishnan led the commando operation launched on 27 November 2008 to flush out terrorists from Hotel Taj Mahal, Mumbai in which he rescued fourteen hostages. During the operation, his team came under intense hostile fire, in which one of his team members got grievously injured. Major Sandeep pinned down the terrorists with accurate fire and rescued the injured commando to safety. In the process, he was shot in his right arm. Despite his injuries, he continued to fight the terrorists till his last breath. Major Sandeep Unnikrishnan displayed most conspicuous bravery besides camaraderie and leadership of the highest order and made the supreme sacrifice for the nation.

* * *

In the early hours of their bereavement, Unnikrishnan, now seventy, and Dhanalakshmi appeared to be experiencing their shared agony in two distinct, only slightly intersecting spheres. Among the thousands visiting them to offer condolences were political leaders from across the region. At one point, the tired, grieving father had an emotional outburst, caught on camera at the gate of his house, amid an exchange of angry comments with a visiting politician. To those watching on millions of television screens across India, it seemed that a gentle, self-effacing man had suddenly been introduced to an unfamiliar part of himself. The mother seemed more and more fragile every day, disbelief and devastation giving way to a vacant exhaustion.

But within the week, by the early days of December 2008, they were a single, solid unit, undertaking an expedition of sorts to retrace Sandeep's journey as far back as Frank Anthony Public School in Bangalore where he'd spent fourteen years, and as proximate as the tidy room he'd left behind at the NSG hub in Manesar when he set out on Operation Black Tornado.

They resolved to find out for themselves exactly where and under what precise circumstances Sandeep had become a martyr. And to comprehend how their son had come to be at the Palm Lounge of the Taj Mahal Palace hotel at that very moment, years of learning and living having apparently led him exactly there. The decision was made about three days after his death. The air thick with the unbearable agony of life ahead with no son, no nine-to-five job, nobody particularly needing them, the ageing couple talked quietly late into the night, discussing how, and whether, they would live without Sandeep. Unnikrishnan told his wife he'd support whatever decision she took.

'We thought deeply. I told him Sandeep had done such a brave thing, we couldn't be cowardly,' Dhanalakshmi recounts. 'Every minute and every second, for the rest of our lives, we will see Sandeep.'

And so it began, a journey with their son's ashes in an urn. They would eventually go to Haridwar, where a bevy of priests broke down with them. But before they bid him goodbye, they took a long, tender look at the people and institutions that had helped frame his worldview, and at the scores of lives he had touched.

They started around 6 December, they remember clearly because it was the anniversary of the Babri Masjid demolition. Sandeep's ashes were still at home, though an uncle had taken one urn to Kerala, where they have family. 'We had no definite plans, but we took his ashes and left. And we kept moving, meeting more and more people in various places,' Unnikrishnan says. They visited his alma mater, where a special school assembly was held as tribute. They visited room number 6 of the Oscar squadron at the NDA, home of the 'Olympians', where Sandeep resided as a cadet of the 94th batch.

But most significant, in those early days, was the chance to retrace their son's steps at the Taj, to 'get a feel' of what had happened there through 27 November. 'It was like a pilgrimage,' says Dhanalakshmi. NSG officials walked them through what had happened while Taj staffers held their hands.

The 51 Special Action Group of the National Security Guard, the Black Cats, are the most lethal of India's elite warriors, skilled as much in stealth as in warfare in just about any circumstance. Sandeep, who had completed three Kashmir tours, including a posting on the Siachen glacier, one of the world's most dangerous battlefields, was already an instructor. But he volunteered for the Mumbai operation when NSG men were informally assembled on the night of 26 November 2008 in Manesar.

After day-long operations to make sure hostages, guests and staffers made it out safely, the Tower wing was almost all-clear. It was well past dusk on the evening of 27 November when Sandeep decided to go up into the palace wing to rescue an employee hiding in a data centre office room. The Unnikrishnans heard from NSG commando Sunil Jodha, then twenty-six years old, a first-hand account of what occurred.

Jodha was in hospital in Mumbai, having taken seven bullets, three to the left hand, one to his right palm, two in his right shoulder and one right through his bulletproof jacket, in the chest region. He told the Unnikrishnans he had been with Sandeep, first in a team clearing guest rooms floor by floor and then in the team that had gone up into the heritage wing through the iconic central stairway of the property. They had barely reached the first floor landing when they came under heavy fire from the gunmen, and a critically wounded Jodha had to be extricated to safety by his team members. Jodha said he owed his life to Sandeep, his mentor. In fact, Sandeep's last instruction to the team had been to stand back as he bounded up the stairway alone, last words that likely saved the lives of all the others in the team.

Further nuggets of information continued to seep out over the next couple of years, pieces of a complex puzzle falling into place as the grieving parents tried to make sense of their loss. On the first anniversary of the attacks, the couple went back to the Taj, now restored and refurbished. They knew that a marble plaque had been installed in the central hall of the heritage wing of the hotel commemorating those who had lost their lives there. 'As soon as we were told about this, we immediately wanted to see it,' says Unnikrishnan.

On 27 November 2009, they sat in prayer at the very spot where Sandeep had been killed. 'The Taj management helped us in every way. The spot is next to a restaurant. They emptied it out. And we could sit for as many hours as we wanted,' says Unnikrishnan.

As he sat in silence, he could sense somebody seated directly behind him. A short while later, the man spoke up—he had been among the last guests to be rescued that night as the hotel burnt and the standoff between the NSG and the gunmen escalated.

The guest had heard the occupant of the neighbouring room in the heritage wing pleading that he was a British citizen, and then being shot anyway. He had heard the rattling bursts an automatic weapon being fired at very close quarters, and grenades exploding a little further away. Certain he was next, he had dragged the bed against the door of the room. So when there was a knock on the door on the night of 27th, after previous knocks, he stayed silent in the pitch-black room. Again, a gentle knock and the words, 'Police, police, police.' Still uncertain, he heard a voice at the door say they would be blasting the door down with a charge and that the guest may or may not survive. Paralysed with fear, he stayed silent. The voice asked if he imagined that Pakistani terrorists spoke English in that accent. 'We are the NSG,' the person at the door told the frightened man who had peered out of his window repeatedly over the past twenty-four hours, seeing with every glance disturbed and horrified faces in the distance, of fire-fighters, some journalists and security forces. 'Then I opened the door and my hours of shock evaporated in an instant—he was so calm,' the guest told Unnikrishnan. It was Sandeep at the door, asking if the guest was hurt, was he alone, did he want anything. From his flak jacket, Sandeep drew out a sachet of water and an apple. The guest requested that he be allowed to take his laptop with him. A commando checked the device with a metal detector and handed it back. Minutes later, he was ensconced in a police vehicle outside, his sole meeting with the men who saved his life having lasted all of a couple of minutes.

The guest, who now remains in touch with Unnikrishnan and addresses him as 'uncle', was overcome with emotion that day in 2009 on meeting the parents of the martyred soldier. 'Repeatedly through that day and night, he had expected to be shot dead,' says Unnikrishnan. Hours later, his protector was dead. 'Such is the treacherous nature of life.'

Those run-ins with the people who helped unravel Sandeep's story for them were only the beginning of the Unnikrishnans' journey. Over the last ten years, they've built lasting relationships from these explorations of his last hours and from deep diving into his life. A young Army wife in Mumbai sought them out on one of their annual visits to the Taj Mahal Hotel, and what began as a polite and respectful expression of solidarity with the parents of a national martyr became a strong bond. She recently lost her husband, also a major, under tragic circumstances and the couple responded by drawing her closer still. 'She's like a daughter to us now,' Unnikrishnan says.

Another new friend, a guest rescued by Sandeep at the Taj, is in the hospitality industry. He invited the couple to spend a weekend at a luxury resort on the west coast. Dhanalakshmi made *aapams* there one afternoon, her first and solitary venture commandeering a five-star kitchen. A guest had asked for them and the kitchen had to send its apologies. 'When she found out, she just volunteered to make them. Aapams are difficult to predict—with the exact same ingredients you can get different results each time. But luckily they turned out great that day. There were happy guests,' says Unnikrishnan, eyes gleaming with pride.

* * *

The top floor of the Unnikrishnans' home is a shrine to a hero. Outside the room, on the facade of the modest two-storey home, is a sign that says 'Major Sandeep Unnikrishnan Memorial Trust'.

Inside, simple cabinets of wood and glass line all four walls, holding the Ashok Chakra, a medal from the Army chief, four service medals, every single trophy and shield Sandeep won through his school and NDA years, scores of photographs, paintings and art work sent in by fans across India and dozens of his personal belongings, every gleaming item suggestive of daily care and polishing. The photographs of Sandeep date back to him as a toddler, as a gangly teen, in uniform. The glass-fronted cupboards hold neatly pressed Army uniforms and fatigues, rows of shoes, even a little muslin shirt he wore when he was barely a year old. His personal effects from his room in Manesar are there too, a half-used tube of toothpaste, shaving cream and deodorant. His wallet left behind at the NSG hub, a couple of hundred-rupee notes inside, is also placed alongside.

There are memories and back-stories with almost every item, and Dhanalakshmi narrates them as she walks along the cabinets, fingers grazing the glass. 'In that photograph there, in which he's sleeping with his head in my lap, he just put his head down and drifted into very sound sleep immediately. He'd just come back from a posting.' She knows which of the dozens of brass cups were won for high jump, which medals for athletics. An ageing desktop PC is in a corner, Sandeep's computer, still in working condition. Collectibles from his postings in Kashmir and Rajasthan. Cards and photo-frames and posters he collected. His DVD collection. She has no explanation for why she hung on to some of these items, his baby clothes, for instance. 'I don't know. I always knew Sandeep was special, but why did I keep these things that are thirty–forty years old?'

In a way, the gallery is the parents' attempt to tell the story of Sandeep's growing-up years.

It was a simple upbringing in a somewhat conservative household, Sandeep growing up with a cousin who also lived with them. There was no real disciplinarian at home, Unnikrishnan turning into a friend Sandeep could confide in or feed eagles with or pluck ripe mangoes with while on holiday in Kerala. By the time Sandeep was ten or twelve years old, Bangalore was already emblematic of a new, aspirational India. All around him in Frank Anthony Public School, where he did fourteen years of his pre-National Defence Academy education, were boyhood daydreams of high-paying jobs at TCS or Infosys and foreign stints to write code. But by Class VIII, Sandeep was wearing his hair in a crew cut, and he had told friends he wanted to join the armed forces. His parents wouldn't know until a couple of years later.

'A top student, he began to slow down in academics somewhere between classes X and XII. I was restless, for we were keen that he become an engineer,' says Unnikrishnan. 'Unknown to me, he was working hard on his extra curriculars, with a plan to get into the NDA.' Those years saw Sandeep excel in sports, with a high-jump record at Frank Anthony that remains unbeaten to date.

The Unnikrishnans don't know what led to his career choice. A very distant relative is a jawan, but hardly somebody Sandeep would have been inspired by. Unnikrishnan himself once showed up at an Indian Army recruitment drive in Cheruvannur in Kozhikode, Kerala. His father had just lost his job and, prompted by circumstances, the young Unnikrishnan had applied, on a whim, only to be rejected as too skinny. Sandeep didn't ever know that.

'I don't know how he grew to feel so strongly about serving the nation,' says the father, a diminutive man who speaks with an easy honesty. 'We brought him up with my own simple theories—don't tell lies, don't disturb others, don't borrow.' But it's easy to see where the young Sandeep picked up his tenacity. Unnikrishnan, who retired from the Indian Space Research Organisation (ISRO), was only a teenager when he'd been forced to take a break from his studies and find a job. Right after Class X, he'd taken courses in secretarial practice and found a job as a secretary, first at Blue Star and then at Sudarshan Trading Co. before joining ISRO. He then completed his PUC (pre-university course) and subsequently his graduation while working full-time.

'Qualification is not everything, a real willingness to work has to be there,' he says now, recounting occasional visits he still makes to the ISRO headquarters in Bangalore. 'Every time I'm there, I still feel that I am going to work. We used to work extra hours so often. I remember we once worked seventy-two hours straight; that was for the launch of INSAT 1A. And from chairman or vice-chairman or group heads to the rest of us, we all had the same level of commitment.' It was that dedication he recognized in Sandeep.

A large section of the gallery is dedicated to his three years in the NDA, an institution that inspired him enough to aspire to return one day as instructor. While his parents had initially balked at the idea of Sandeep joining the armed forces, once he was in the NDA, they visited him on every holiday and found themselves swept up in his enthusiasm. 'We'd see cadets dozing while standing in a bus from Khadakvasla to Pune, they worked that hard,' laughs Unnikrishnan. 'We were totally supportive. It was beginning to be obvious to us that he was meant to do this. He wanted to achieve something.'

Needless to say, there are photographs of his passing out parade. Dhanalakshmi remembers the day he came home after being commissioned as an officer, back in 1999, when he sat his parents down and told them gravely that the unit, 7 Bihar Regiment, was now his family. 'I would never say he is the best soldier in the world. In fact, in his regiment, I have seen more vigour and fearlessness. But he was the most dedicated,' says Unnikrishnan.

They show visitors around the gallery with pride, Dhanalakshmi's eyes moistening as she picks out items, giving some a quick wipe before putting them back, talking tirelessly about Sandeep. They've had all kinds of visitors—journalists, politicians, local residents, those seeking aid through the trust. At other times, groups of Sandeep's former colleagues, juniors or even armymen from across India have shown up, wanting to see the gallery and requesting a meal. Once a choir group came on Christmas Eve, electronic synthesizer and music notes in hand. If it's for Sandeep, they turn nobody away.

The Sandeep Unnikrishnan Memorial Trust was set up in March 2009, inspired by MP Rajeev Chandrashekhar who donated Rs 25 lakh. Initially they began offering aid to various people in need, including medical assistance. The trust now focuses on educating young girls who show an inclination to study further, selecting those with test scores indicating an ability to do well but whose conditions at home are difficult.

One case is exemplary, of a Class IX student who scored between ninety-five and 100 in five subjects at last year's final exams. Residents of a remote village in Kanakapura taluka, about 55 km from Bangalore, the family had actually approached the Unnikrishnans seeking assistance with medical expenses for the younger child, a boy, who had a malignant brain tumour. 'The mother herself was just a child, she'd been married off at thirteen and had become a mother at fifteen,' says Unnikrishnan. She'd nearly pulled the girl out of school when the Unnikrishnans asked to see her mark sheet. 'There were safety concerns as girls in the village have to walk a long distance and then board a bus to get to school. The girl is now in a residential school in Mangalore. We will spend on her right till she completes her higher education,' he says. This June, the trust handed her a first cheque of Rs 35,000 for the current academic year.

Another case is the daughter of a single mother who operates a small laundry service. The trust has been paying the school fees of the child, now in Class II, for the last two years.

Over the past three or four years, the Unnikrishnans decided that's what they would like to focus on, helping girls who need a little nudge in completing their education. Sandeep would have done just that, they say. For he was forever inclined to help out, even at some cost to himself. In 2007, when Dhanalakshmi's ancestral property in their village in Kerala was to be divided among four siblings, Sandeep called to say she should forfeit her share. 'We don't need it, he said. I had wanted to be able to leave it for him, but he would have none of it,' she remembers. So in December 2007, Sandeep came home and the two made the trip to Kerala, to sign off her claim on the land. 'Sandeep would tell me there's a world beyond these four walls. People have problems I know nothing of, he would say.'

* * *

In response to their simple overtures to the country, over the last ten years, the Unnikrishnans have been repeatedly overwhelmed at the outpouring of support and emotion from strangers.

This summer, Unnikrishnan was returning home on Route 333 of the Vajra bus service operated by Bangalore Metropolitan Transport Corporation. As the bus halted at the Kadugodi flyover, he prepared to alight—he would need a connecting bus from the terminal. The conductor told me not to alight, to wait comfortably inside the bus for the next one. He said he knows me, and that he wanted to do this. I eventually refused, but it was touching. It's not that they know me, but they know Sandeep, they recognize what he did,' says the father.

On another occasion, they were waiting at New Delhi railway station to board a train back home to Bangalore when an announcement said their train would now depart from another platform. Within minutes, a group of soldiers, most of them Haryanvi, gathered around the couple, picked up their bags and began the long walk across the platform and up the stairs. Once at the right spot to board, bags double-checked and lined up, they got talking with the Unnikrishnans. They were headed to Tirunelveli, in Tamil Nadu. They'd recognized the couple immediately, and said they thought it was a privilege to be able to assist Major Sandeep Unnikrishnan's parents. 'In the course of the conversation, one of them also said something else that I will always remember,' says Unnikrishnan. 'Once he donned the uniform, he felt he was a new person. He believed that there will be nobody with him at the end, just his *vardi*. Soldiers are like that.'

For a couple in their late sixties and seventies, Unnikrishnan and Dhanalakshmi are incredibly busy. Even an Ayurveda regime for her had to wait months because either somebody was visiting, or they had to be in another town, or a relative had a minor accident. At sixty-six, Dhanalakshmi prefers not to employ any domestic help, still keeping the simple two-storey house gleaming, the rows and rows of potted plants with flowers and exotic medicinal herbs lush and inviting.

From unveiling statues of Sandeep to talking about his martyrdom at events, the couple goes wherever they are invited. But grief, even when they're not discussing their loss, is ever present. A proud grief, but no less tormenting, and one that has changed the way they view their world, made them reconsider the small details. They say they've repeatedly circled through the events leading up to that moment, coming to the same conclusion every time that there can be no real explanation for why they were chosen for this searing grief. But both say they've worked to make sure they're neither catatonic in their suffering nor emotionally spent and empty.

Sandeep was to return home in December 2008. On the agenda for that holiday was teaching his mother to drive. That was not to be. Then, in 2010, to mark the second anniversary of the attacks, Unnikrishnan joined a cycling enthusiast from Mumbai to ride 1600 km on a bicycle from New Delhi to the Taj in Mumbai. On that journey Dhanalakshmi followed in a car, but by 2012 she had learnt to ride and completed a cycle yatra as a tribute to martyrs.

The lurking grief means they will think of him suddenly. While watching the rice boil because he'd often want his mother to feed him, thrusting little bits of rice and curry into his mouth with her fingers. Or when she's picking out a saree because Sandeep was so particular about how neat her sarees's pleats were. A particular route in Bangalore will remind the couple of Unnikrishnan's 20-km drive to fetch fried sardines that Sandeep loved to eat with his tea. And yet, ten years have been spent making mindful contributions, finding new purpose. 'God has given me something special, that my son is special,' Dhanalakshmi says.

This year on 15 March, like every year since 2008, a few hundred people gathered outside their home for an hour-long tribute on Sandeep's birthday. He would have turned forty-one this year. The couple also sent out a few hundred customized cards with Sandeep's photo on the top and inside, against a backdrop of the Indian flag. 'Salute to you on your forty-first birthday,' it said. A *pandal* and food were organized by the Unnikrishnans, and a local organization took over the task of putting together a befitting memorial. Dhanalakshmi says, '*Logon ke man mein Sandeep hai*. He's in their minds even now. That's all we live for.'

Somnath Hore, *Untitled,* etching and engraving, 1983
Collection: DAG

2

Living with Mental Trauma

Tabassum Barnagarwala

No two days have ever been the same since that night. In ten years, Govind Singh Kathayat has found himself running, at great speed, through a range of emotions ranging from turmoil to emptiness, fear to anger. He has had hallucinations and suicidal thoughts, many times over. For two terrifying nights, he was stuck inside a restaurant behind the Taj Mahal Palace and Tower Hotel, the sound of gunfire and grenades making them cower in the dark. A glimpse of the Taj's burning dome had made him certain that he wouldn't make it out alive.

Now forty, Govind says it is only in the last year that he has found some peace, a comfortable rhythm. Wearing thick glasses, he lowers his somewhat bulky frame into a plastic chair in his home in Thane, just on the outskirts of Mumbai. Govind smiles brightly. His mother is thrilled at his recent weight gain. Beside him, tightly swaddled, is his son Chaitanya, not yet one year old and enjoying an unperturbed nap on a thin mat thrown on the tiled floor. Govind crosses his legs, and his right hand hovers near Radha, his wife of less than two years. The rains have just arrived and the sudden cool air floods their simple suburban apartment, lifting everyone's mood. The family is almost beaming. A new life has begun, it seems.

'I can finally say it's all in the past now. I never thought I would be sitting and talking normally like this,' Govind begins. Radha smiles. 'She has been my biggest support over the past year.'

Between 28 November 2008, when he was rescued from his hideout, and 2014, Govind had to be hospitalized seven times for mental illness, battling clinical depression and schizophrenia that appeared to have been triggered by his ordeal. He spent two nights inside the Busaba restaurant tucked away in a lane behind the Taj, where he worked as an accounts manager. He was thirty then, with a four-month-old son Rajeev and a wife, Rama, who worked as a tuition teacher.

In the decade since, Govind saw his marriage crumble, lost access to his son and saw his job slip away as he battled mental illness. It was only in 2014 that he somehow managed to extricate himself from the shackles of 26/11, and started looking for a new job and a new life partner.

The bedroom can barely hold five people. A single divan-bed with a hollow storage space is pushed up against a wall. Two iron almirahs stand against the opposite wall and two plastic chairs in between offer extra seating for guests. A tiny passage leads to the kitchen where steel racks hold utensils. On a black stone platform sits a two-burner gas stove. The only other room is the living room, which doubles up at night into Govind's parents' bedroom. The family has lived here for sixteen years.

Govind and Radha were married on 14 May 2017, a month after they first met in Bageshwar, a town in their native state of Uttarakhand. It was a simple ceremony at a local temple in Bageshwar, with only Govind's family and Radha's closest relatives in attendance. Both had one failed marriage behind them, and were clear that they didn't want another grand wedding ceremony.

'When we met, he told me everything about his past life. We shared a common pain, I realized,' Radha says. Govind's mother interjects, 'We had decided not to hide anything about his mental illness. What is the sense in hiding it?'

In April 2017, it had been two years since he was discharged from Thane Mental Hospital. Govind had managed to settle into a job in Dadar, central Mumbai. His father, Kundan Singh Kathayat, a retired Indian Navy sailor, and his mother, Bhagirathi, thought the time was apt for him to get married again. All three of them travelled to Bageshwar, a three-and-a-half-hour bus ride from Nainital. They had seen photographs of a prospective bride, and were hopeful of finalizing an alliance.

But they'd barely reached Bageshwar when they received a curt phone call informing them that the meeting would have to be called off. 'That girl's brother had met with an accident. So they were superstitious about Govind,' Bhagirathi says. The same day, an acquaintance at a local shop casually mentioned that his niece, recently divorced, was looking to marry again. 'We decided to meet her the same day.' Bhagirathi was impulsive, and also stubborn; she did not want to return to Mumbai without a bride for Govind.

They drove ten minutes to a nearby village with barely forty ramshackle homes, where Govind first met Radha, then thirty-five, on 3 April 2017.

Radha's first marriage had been to an armyman, seven years her senior, in 2007. Her family had been keen to find a government employee who enjoyed a secure job. 'He would beat me and abuse me after drinking,' she says. Divorced in 2017, she began to teach in Bageshwar. She had completed a bachelors in education and later an MA in history. Her family started looking out for prospective grooms. 'But I rejected government employees this time,' she says.

When she met Govind, both realized they shared a pain—an unhappy marriage and a subsequent divorce. Govind told her about the terror attack of 2008, of how he developed anxiety and depression following the attack and then lost his wife and job to his mental illness.

Radha told him about her first marriage, and about the domestic violence she suffered for ten years. Both had, for a decade, undergone an onerous phase.

'I can understand only two types of mental illnesses: one where the person is out of control and dangerous, and the other where he is able to live life with some support. Back in the village we never witnessed any terrorist attack, so I can never understand his anguish of having survived that. But I knew I could live with him,' Radha says. He offered her no promise of an adventurous life in the big city—he was still emerging from years of battling mental illness. But she knew that together they could build a life for themselves. And one month later, in a temple close to her house, the two tied the knot; Radha in a red sari and Govind in a magenta sherwani.

In February 2018, their son Chaitanya was born.

* * *

It was 9 a.m., his usual time, when Govind left his house in Manpada, in the western part of Thane city, to catch a bus to the Thane railway station on 26 November 2008. From there a fast train brought him to Chhatrapati Shivaji Terminus station. A short ten-minute share-cab ride away, the two-storey Busaba restaurant stood in plush Colaba's Mandlik Road. The entire journey from his home to the quaint office in South Mumbai took two hours.

The Southeast Asian restaurant was inaugurated on 22 September 2001, in a bungalow located in a leafy lane behind the Taj Mahal Palace hotel. On its ground floor stood a rectangular bar with a high wooden counter and dim red lights overhead. Spanning the floor were low-slung plush chairs and wooden tabletops. A side staircase to the first floor opened into a long passage that housed the restaurant. Busaba's owner and chef Nikhil Chib had travelled extensively through Southeast Asia. So when he opened the restaurant, he made sure the menu had a versatile mix of Vietnamese, Thai, Korean and Myanmarese delicacies.

In the bungalow-turned-restaurant, Govind's office was on the second floor, adjoining a storeroom. 'I would manage the accounts there. Four people worked under me,' he says.

That day, he remembers, there was a pile of documents he had to finish assessing. By 8 p.m., when Govind normally left for home, he was still buried under work. His juniors had left by 6 p.m. In the tiny office space on the second floor, only Govind and the general manager, Gary Saldanha, remained.

It was shortly after 9.30 p.m. when Govind looked up from his work, his irritation mounting at the constant noise of what he thought were firecrackers. Saldanha ignored it too. 'Weddings were common at the Taj hotel. Gary and I thought this was another wedding. It was only when I saw people running towards our restaurant that I realized something was wrong,' Govind recollects.

Outside, there was absolute panic and mayhem. Some people were running towards them from the direction of Leopold Cafe. Soon after, people were fleeing from another direction, away from the Taj hotel. Several people, Govind noticed, were missing one or both pieces of footwear. 'People said there was a shootout in Leopold and inside Taj. We switched on the TV then.'

It took the better part of an hour for the situation to sink in. Coordinated terrorist attacks had been launched at multiple locations across Mumbai. The CST train station, where Govind had alighted only this morning, was among them. It then dawned on them that the rattling and popping bursts of sound from the Taj Mahal hotel were actually gunshots.

The Busaba restaurant had a capacity to hold about thirty–forty guests. That night, over sixty took refuge in the dimly lit building. Security guards switched off lights on the first and second floors. A dim red light continued to light the lounge on the ground floor where most of the guests had taken refuge.

'I am a person who can be worried very easily. But somehow I passed the first night without expressing fear,' Govind remembers. He called his elder sister and let her know that he'd stay back in the restaurant for the night. 'We only had the television to know what was going on. Our elder daughter stayed over with us, assuring us every few minutes that Govind would be back safe the next day,' says Bhagirathi.

From the security cabin of Busaba, Govind saw the heritage building of the Taj look fearsome as the siege continued. The Busaba management believed in ordering in fresh supplies every day. That night, the staff cooked whatever was available to serve the crowd dinner. But there were no supplies the following morning.

Through 27–28 November, the nearly sixty refugees packed into Busaba survived on water. The attack continued inside the Taj and Mandlik Road remained cordoned off. Soon, Govind's cell-phone battery died and he would have to wait for his turn to make a call home from the landline.

By mid-day on the 27th, despair seeped in all around. Govind has only one phrase to describe the mood inside their hideout: *'Dehshat bhara mahaul'*, (an atmosphere of terror). They watched, shocked, as a portion of the main red dome of the Taj exploded, pieces of stone flying in every direction. The fire that followed spewed smoke for hours into the night. 'After a few hours, we couldn't remember the date or time. It just went on,' he says.

Over ten years, Govind's memory of the attack has faded a little. Nevertheless, he stammers with apparent fear when he speaks about it. 'I think I stepped out on the morning of 28 November. A policeman from Colaba came to inform us that it was safe to step out.'

Chef and owner Chib had arranged taxis for his employees. Govind was taken to his Thane home, 42 km away. Until then, Govind remembers speaking to everybody as normally as possible and hugging his colleagues in relief at having emerged alive.

'When he returned he asked us to draw all the curtains and lock the door. He wanted absolute darkness. We thought it was natural to be scared,' his father, Kundan Singh Kathayat, says. But over the next three days, they could see something was seriously wrong. Govind would keep repeating that he was afraid someone would kill him.

He didn't know it then, but depression had set in.

He was not alone in his fear. Chib says two of his security guards also faced a traumatic period after the attacks. 'They asked to go on leave. Our restaurant remained shut, so did almost all of Colaba, for about four days I believe,' Chib says. Then, as Mumbai bounced back, Busaba opened its gates to diners by the fifth day after the attack ended. Three years ago, the restaurant shut its Colaba operations and shifted to Lower Parel.

The Tata Trust, which has been aiding survivors of the terror attack and victims' families since 2008, found that most victims required medical support. Soon after the attacks, the Trust started a centre in Andheri, in Mumbai's western suburbs, where doctors would provide regular psychological support to victims of the 2006 Mumbai serial train explosions and the 2008 terror attacks. 'That helped bring several out of trauma. But most, I saw, needed medical attention. Even now, several victims suffer from hypertension and diabetes. The attack is related to their current condition,' says Agnes Martis, attached with the Tata Trust.

* * *

Located adjoining the railway tracks laid for India's very first train system that ran from Mumbai to Thane, the Thane Mental Hospital is housed on a lush campus of 60 acres. The 1850-bed facility is one of four government-run mental health institutions in Maharashtra.

In its large wards spread across the leafy premises, the hospital admits patients with mental retardation, bipolar disorder, schizophrenia, depression and those with suicidal tendencies. About 40 per cent of the patients here have been living in the hospital for years, having faced permanent abandonment by their immediate families. There is also a separate wing with individual cells for prisoners suffering from mental illnesses. Also located on campus is an outpatient department where doctors check over 200 patients daily.

In September 2010, Govind quit his job in Busaba and told his parents he wants to get admitted to Thane Mental Hospital. By then he had already tried, and been disappointed by, several treatment options. Within a month of the attacks, Govind had visited the Institute for Psychological Help (IPH) in Naupada, Thane West. The institute offers psychological support and focuses mostly on patients with depression. Govind was prescribed half a dozen medicines. 'But my problem only grew after taking those medicines. I couldn't sleep. And if I did, I had bad dreams. I could not look anyone in the eye,' he says.

Between 2008 and 2010, Kundan took Govind to homeopathic doctors. They tried visiting saints and self-professed miracle healers, and conducted poojas in various temples, hoping to find a cure. 'We would come to know of some miraculous saint in some remote village and we would take him there,' Kundan recollects.

There were times when Govind lost all hope. In his medical records, doctors write that he attempted suicide three times. Once, he mixed whiskey with an insect repellant. On another occasion, he cut his wrist.

The decision to get himself hospitalized came after his wife left him, taking with her their two-year-old son Rajeev. 'I would miss my son terribly. She would not let me meet him. I didn't know what was happening to my life. I never thought I would become normal again,' he says.

It was 28 June 2010, when he first visited the Thane hospital's outpatient department. 'The initial findings were complaints of anxiety, irritability, occasional anger and lack of sleep,' says psychiatrist Dr Sandeep Divekar of the hospital.

Govind was diagnosed with anxiety disorder and psychosis. He was put on medication for sleep and anxiety control. On 10 January 2011, he was admitted to the mental hospital for the first time where he stayed for two months. In July 2012, he underwent the Minnesota Multiphasic Personality Inventory (MMPI) test—a psychological test that assesses personality traits and psychopathology—at the Lokmanya Tilak Municipal General Hospital in Sion, in central Mumbai. 'The reading came as 295.3—the code for paranoid schizophrenia,' Dr Divekar says.

Medical records from Thane Mental Hospital show that until 2014 Govind required multiple admissions. In February 2013, he was admitted for the second time with angry outbursts and uncontrolled fear. He was discharged on 4 April, only to be readmitted a week later for two months.

On 14 August 2013, his father brought him back for a month-long hospitalization. In 2014, he was admitted three times, each time for three months. His last hospitalization was on 30 September 2014 when he remained in hospital till 28 November. It was incidentally also the exact day, six years previously, that he had been rescued from Busaba. That was the last time he saw Ward Number 19, which had become his second home. The ward, he says, gave him more comfort than the world outside during his worst phase as he battled illness.

He smiles as he recollects the names of his two best friends in the hospital: one an almost childlike man who suffered from severe mental retardation, and another with bipolar disorder.

Govind remembers the number of electric shocks he was administered through twelve sessions. But in the hospital, away from his estranged wife and family, Govind found a new home, a new routine. 'It felt safer, confined within the four walls,' he says.

His day would begin at 5 a.m. The hospital would make use of its fit patients to serve those who could not do their own chores. Govind would bring tea and serve it to the other inpatients every morning. At 6 a.m., he would help them bathe. By 8 a.m., along with ward boys, he would distribute medicines to patients and then head to the occupational therapy room to work on a computer. 'I kept my contact with the computer, hoping that one day I'll resume work and may need my computer skills,' he says. A ward boy everyone referred to as Solanki looked after

Govind. He knew when Govind needed his medicines and what mood swings he had.

Slowly, Govind let go of his shyness, helped along by the bond with his two new friends. The three would wash utensils together, and later by 4 p.m. every day they would serve tea to the other patients. A second round of medicines followed, to be administered by 6 p.m., before dinner at 8 p.m.

There were difficult times too. 'Sometimes ward boys would threaten to make us do more menial tasks such as clean the toilets, asking us to get money from our families,' Govind alleges. His father adds, 'He told us about that several times. But fighting with the hospital staff made no sense. My son was admitted there.' The hospital has maintained that it is sensitizing its staff members to treat patients well.

While India has a Disaster Management Protocol, it does not delve too deep into socio-psychological support required by the victims of terror attacks or natural disasters. 'In the USA and European countries, there is a system to establish contact with the victim from day one, and to keep providing them counselling and social support. If there is a need, psychiatric counselling is regularly given. India lacks resources, and with our population it is difficult to implement the counselling component,' says Dr Shubhangi Parkar, head of the psychiatry department at the busy KEM Hospital.

KEM Hospital, run by the Brihanmumbai Municipal Corporation, receives the largest burden of patients with mental illnesses among all Mumbai hospitals. Between 2015 and 2017, for instance, 1.01 lakh patients came with psychiatric disorders. In comparison, 69,752 patients were registered as suffering from hypertension, making mental illness the most common medical ailment that the hospital currently treats. 'But to address the huge load, we need a strong primary healthcare system,' says Dr Avinash Supe, dean at KEM Hospital.

Dr Parkar—who has been actively counselling those injured in a stampede at the Elphinstone Road railway station in 2017, in which twenty-three people died—adds that immediate family support is the basic requirement to ensure that survivors are able to face the world again. 'After that, comes the role of planned services such as counselling, regular follow-ups and social support,' she says.

According to her, the idea is to remove insecurity and assure such patients that a normal life is possible. India needs more specialists to ensure a systemic response to post-trauma stress among survivors of terror attacks.

Govind, for instance, has the support of his family. His doctor in Thane Mental hospital adds that the personal support he received helped hugely in him winning the battle over depression. Since 2014, though he did not require hospitalization, Govind has attended a counselling session every month without fail. 'In his case, his parents have shown immense support. He has managed to stay out of the hospital for a long time now. Most mentally ill patients are abandoned by their families,' Dr Divekar says.

For Govind, who now requires medication to sleep and to control anxiety, it is possible to lead a normal life.

'But he'll require lifelong medication,' his doctor adds. 'If he can confide in his employer about his past treatment, their empathy may further help him professionally.'

* * *

Seated on a bench at the Airport Road metro station, a short walk from his new employer's address in Andheri East, Govind is unperturbed by the crowd around him. Some years ago, he would have been agitated, drawing drapes down, switching off lights to remain in total darkness. 'I never thought that one day I will stand on my feet again. I was conscious but I could do nothing, as if I were dead,' he says. 'The credit for what I am today goes to my dad. He would keep me engaged during my depressed phase, making me go pay utility bills, or do his bank work.'

He last saw his son Rajeev in 2010 when his relationship with Rama, his first wife, turned sour. She felt like she could no longer live with him, he says, adding that their separation lacerated his bond with his son. Over the years, he made several attempts to meet Rajeev, but with little success. In 2012, consumed by despair, he went to Rama's home nearby. 'She gave tuitions in the evening. When I went, she refused to talk to me. I switched off the main electric meter so that she would be forced to come out.' A fight ensued, followed by a police complaint of harassment.

In December 2013, Govind signed the divorce papers at the Thane family court.

After his final discharge from the hospital in 2014, he started looking for employment through online job portals. He got through at the very first application he sent, finding work at a chemical-manufacturing unit in Lower Parel. But within a month, he was asked to leave. He then worked in Worli at a food-manufacturing unit. A month later, he quit.

'It was a difficult period. I realized that the world is more competitive, more skilled than it was five–six years earlier,' he says. In Thane Mental Hospital, he would often use the computer to hone his accounting skills, hoping that the practice would help. But he realized as he made a comeback that the skill set he needed was far more challenging than what was required of him at Busaba.

Govind then joined a plastic-manufacturing company in Vile Parle, where he lasted ten months. He switched to a Parsi group in Dadar for the next ten months before joining a company in Mahape, Navi Mumbai, where he lasted four months.

After his second marriage, he joined his current company in Andheri East where he looks after the accounts of at least twenty housing societies.

Psychiatrists in the Thane Mental Hospital observe that Govind will still need time to adjust in a new environment, even as medicines keep his anxiety in check. 'He needs a supervisor who is understanding and gives him enough time to finish work.' Dr Divekar says. But Govind is optimistic. 'I did not even imagine this much for myself,' he smiles.

With Radha, he says, his confidence has shot up. He earns Rs 45,000 every month. She ensures he takes his three medicines on time.

She wakes up by 6 a.m. every day and cooks his lunch along with his mother. He leaves home by 8.30 a.m., his son Chaitanya invariably playful around that time. By 9 p.m. when he usually returns, Chaitanya is ready to play some more. 'He has filled the gap I felt when I lost access to my first son. It is hard to believe, but I don't think about him now as often as I did,' Govind says.

Chittaprosad, *Untitled*, graphite on paper, 1943
Collection: DAG

3

A Man the Nation Owes

Mayura Janwalkar

It was a Wednesday. Assistant Police Inspector Tukaram Omble was scheduled to work the evening shift. The television was tuned to the cricket match—India was playing England in the fifth ODI of a seven match bilateral cricket series in Cuttack. Before he could leave for the DB Marg police station to report to work, the cricket buff checked the score on the television. Even afterwards, he kept calling home to get an update on the score.

'He had called at least twice or thrice to ask for the score,' says Vaishali, third of Omble's four daughters. 'But after 9 o'clock we heard that something had gone wrong at the VT (CSMT) station and at the Taj Hotel. When Pappa called again, I was a bit irritated. *Ata jinkli na* India? *Parat parat kai* phone *kartay* (Hasn't India won now? Why do you keep calling)? I said. But then he told me that there was an attack in South Mumbai. He told me, my mother and my sisters to stay indoors.'

When she asked him how the situation at DB Marg police station was, he said nothing had happened in their area until then. And then, fully familiar with her father's alacrity in staying at the front at all times, she cautioned him, 'I know you are in the habit of staying at the front but please be careful,' she said. He told her he would.

After that, calls made to his phone went unanswered. The moment that made him a national hero was not witnessed by his family. They would be told later that he had made the ultimate sacrifice, making sure even as he braved bullets that one terrorist was captured alive on the night of 26 November 2008. About 5 km from where Omble died, his wife and daughters waited for his call. And in the years since they continued to live in the long shadow of the night when he never returned home.

* * *

That this martyr's village hasn't forgotten him is immediately apparent upon driving into Kedambe, a village of about 250 homes separated by paddy fields framed by lush hill slopes, 284 km from Mumbai. A banner bearing the photograph of Assistant Police Inspector Tukaram Omble who was killed while capturing terrorist Ajmal Kasab is at the entrance to the village where he grew up, and where his heart always was. 'Shaheed Tukaram Omble', it says, a daily reminder of his martyrdom.

In the primary school where the policeman was once a student, children tell the story of their intrepid hero and his ultimate sacrifice with as much ease as they sing a powada, a traditional Marathi ballad, in praise of Chhatrapati Shivaji Maharaj outwitting Bijapur noble Afzal Khan, a story that has found renditions in Maharashtra's folk music for generations.

In the classroom, the question, 'Who was Tukaram Omble?' is met with an array of answers, all correct. 'He was a policeman,' there is a chorus. Standing among the group of powada singers is ten-year-old Swanand Omble, son of Omble's cousin Ramchandra. He says in a voice barely louder than a whisper, '*Majhya kakanni* Kasab*la pakadla* (my uncle captured Kasab).'

That night in 2008 when Swanand was only a few months old, Tukaram Omble, then fifty-three years old, was in a police bandobast near Girgaum Chowpatty, Mumbai's most iconic beachfront. Wireless messages had said two armed terrorists had carjacked a Skoda sedan and were speeding in their direction. When the car stopped at the bandobast on the mostly deserted road past midnight, Kasab stepped out of the passenger side, his AK-47 pointed at the waiting policemen. Omble threw himself at Kasab, taking a spray of bullets even as he tackled the terrorist to the ground, his sacrifice leading to Kasab being captured alive, and setting the foundation for a long investigation and judicial process that could clearly pin down the conspirators across the border.

But the fact that memories of his bravery live on in the minds of students, many of them born after he was killed, is in itself a special tribute to Omble, who was extremely fond of children.

At the time that he joined the Mumbai Police in 1979, Omble had let go of a job opportunity in the Brihanmumbai Electric Supply and Transport (BEST) undertaking. Drawn to the uniform since he was a boy grazing his cattle, he had always looked up to his maternal aunt's husband, a driver with the Indian Army. Eventually, for the young man who once sold jackfruits and mangoes in Kedambe, the road through the Sahyadri hills out of Satara district to Mumbai was the one that would lead him to his uniform.

It was a proud day for his joint family in the scenic village when he came back as a Mumbai Police constable or, as they still fondly call him, 'hawaldar'. He was the first from his village to don the khaki uniform, but in the ten years since his martyrdom, many more have signed up for jobs as policemen.

Prakash Omble, Kedambe's deputy sarpanch and Omble's first cousin, says, 'He was the first policeman in our village. Since 26/11, there have been thirteen others. Six are posted in Mumbai, four in Pune and some others in the Border Security Force (BSF) and the Indian Navy. A memorial to him in our village continues to inspire the youth.'

Septuagenarian Sulabai Shelar is Omble's niece, but she has memories of them growing up together. 'He would bring so many chocolates every time he came visiting from the city,' she says animatedly. 'And he would give them to all the kids in the village.'

Back in Mumbai, Omble's daughter Vaishali also reminisces about her father's love for children. In a way, he was the Pied Piper of the police residential quarters on Sir Pochkhanawala Road in Worli. 'Whenever he came home after work in the evenings at least two or three kids from the building would follow him home. He was very popular among them,' she says. Minutes later, a neighbour drops off her two-year-old daughter at the Omble residence, the toddler making herself at home almost immediately, finding a cozy corner on the sofa for a quick nap. Their home, Vaishali says, is still accustomed to the presence of children. 'Whenever he had a chance, he would buy food for street kids. He loved children and everything he did for them came straight from the heart,' she says.

In Kedambe, the primary school children look up to Omble. Chandrakant Jadhav, a teacher in the Zilla Parishad School in Kedambe says, 'When we tell these children about patriotism, in Omble we have an example from home.'

The kids may be unsure whether Omble, then attached to the DB Marg police station in Mumbai, nabbed Pakistani terrorist Kasab at Marine Drive or the nearby railway station Marine Lines. But if it was not for Omble's bravery, they believe, Kasab would not have been caught alive. About that, they are absolutely sure.

The village primary school ground has almost all villagers in attendance on days of national importance such as Independence Day and Republic Day. On many such occasions, Tukaram Omble was present with his wife and four daughters, his family remembers. In the decade since his passing, the village has one more important day to observe, its own hero to remember.

'There are three days that are very important to us— 15 August, 26 January and 26 November,' the deputy sarpanch says.

* * *

Driving up the slopes in the Sahyadri mountains, on the foothills of touristy Mahabaleshwar, it comes as no surprise that Omble was hoping to eventually move back to his native village after retiring from Mumbai Police. Kedambe, like many villages off the Pachwad-Medha-Mahabaleshwar road in Satara, is lined with paddy fields. The weather is pleasant, the air crisp and the torrential rains lend the village an air of enigma.

But Kedambe is now known outside Jaoli tehsil as the village of Tukaram Omble, immortalized on plaques, banners, the village school and the shrine of its guardian, Plague Baba.

The legend of Plague Baba dates back to 1896, the year in which the bubonic plague gripped Mumbai, claiming hundreds of lives. 'When the plague broke out in Mumbai, the villagers prayed to the deity and promised to build him a temple if he ensured that the plague did not reach their village. Subsequently, the temple of Plague Baba was built,' says Shankar Omble, the martyred policeman's first cousin. Plague Baba is actually a form of Bhairavnath, an incarnation of Lord Shiva, that the villagers worship.

It was in Plague Baba's temple, deputy sarpanch Prakash says, that Omble spent a large part of his growing-up days. There was another thread that bound Omble to the temple. While he still lived, Omble's father Gopal Omble was the only person in the village tasked with painting and repainting the deity that is mounted on a horse.

'The temple was much smaller back in the day. It had wooden walls. He spent all his time in this temple playing surpatya (a kind of catch-and-cook) and other games that children played,' Prakash says. Located at the very boundary of the village, the Plague Baba shrine, villagers believe, has been the protector of nature, their crops and their values.

For the four Omble sisters in Mumbai, therefore, it was obvious that anything they chose to do in the memory of their father would have to be in Kedambe.

On 17 January 2010, Omble's wife Tarabai and daughters Pavitra, Vandana, Vaishali and Bharti decided to spruce up the temple, make its main hall wider and give it stronger walls. The plaque on the temple wall reads that the groundbreaking ceremony for the temple was carried out by Ananda Kondiba Mhaskar, Omble's schoolteacher, and that the construction of the temple was completed by Tara Tukaram Omble for the fulfilment of her martyred husband's wish and in memory of his parents Gopal Dhondiba Omble and Shevanta Gopal Omble.

Vaishali says the four sisters have also started a charitable trust in his memory that they run using their personal savings. They have donated two of the nine computers in the computer lab of the village primary school. The school teaches children Microsoft Office operations. Students as young as in Class I learn to switch the machines on and off, says school principal Shankar Jambhale. Prakash says his niece has also often donated school bags and books for the children.

Deputy sarpanch Prakash is a civil engineer. He says very soon the village will have its first sports complex, named Shaheed Tukaram Omble Kreeda Sankul. The village vouches for his skills as a kabaddi player his family remembers his love for cricket and carom. 'There are a lot of kids in the village who have the potential to be very good sportspersons. The sports complex we have in mind will also have a swimming pool,' says Prakash.

With a population of about a thousand, Kedambe has a unanimously appointed Gram Panchayat. It does not go to polls. Next to the Plague Baba temple, on a mezzanine floor is the new hall for the seven Panchayat members to meet. That too is now named after Omble.

Omble had two brothers and a sister but like Prakash and Shankar, who introduce themselves as his brothers, in a joint household, kids grow up as siblings and not cousins. 'Nobody here refers to one another as cousins. My cousin is my brother just like my niece is my daughter,' says Shankar. 'Each family has their space in the house but if one of their kids ate or slept in any of the other rooms, nobody even notices,' says Prakash.

50

The home that Omble wanted to retire in has a red roof. It remains locked, except when his wife and daughters come to visit from Mumbai.

The main Bhairavnath temple in Kedambe is on the banks of the Venna, a tributary of the Krishna. Behind the temple is a staircase enveloped in shrubbery that leads to the riverbank, the gurgling of the river water against the rocks a pleasant sound for anyone seated on the steps. The ten-day Ganeshotsav concludes on this riverbank, when villagers immerse idols in the river and bid farewell to their beloved Ganesh deities.

As a retirement plan, Kedambe is ideal, away from urban chaos. But what drew Omble to Kedambe every once in a while is not hard to fathom—in the lap of nature where the river water is icy cold, the people are incredibly warm.

'Whenever we would go back to the village, he would pack a bag this big,' says Omble's wife Tarabai, a woman of few words, stretching out her arms. 'In that bag, his clothes would occupy a tiny space. The rest would be filled with gifts and sweets for everyone in the village,' she says. Tarabai, who hails from Valinjwadi, a village not far from Kedambe, was married to Omble in 1981. Every time he left the village, Omble would be looking forward to returning, a sentiment his family now shares.

* * *

The Plague Baba temple was renovated and inaugurated by Ananda Kondiba Mhaskar, a man Omble held so much in high regard that his family insisted that he would not have preferred anybody else to do the honours. The position he had in Omble's life is evidenced in the place he continues to hold in the minds of the family.

Mhaskar Guruji, as he is commonly referred to in the village, now lives in Sawli village that falls on the way from Pachwad to Kedambe. His two sons live and work in Mumbai and Thane. One of them is now building a spacious new home for his family in the village. Standing at the door of the under-construction duplex overlooking paddy fields is the retired schoolteacher.

Mhaskar Guruji maintains the demeanour of a schoolteacher, stern and pragmatic. But at the mention of Omble's remains being brought back to Kedambe in 2008, the seventy-two-year-old breaks down. 'When they brought his body back to the village, somebody brought me a garland and told me to pay my last respects. What to do you think I felt? He was my student.' He pauses to compose himself. 'Grief,' he says.

As a student, Mhaskar remembers Omble as a very obedient child. 'Whenever I asked him to do anything, he would never say no. He, like many other children in the village, came from a poor family. He was shy and quiet,' says Mhaskar.

When Omble joined Mumbai Police, Mhaskar didn't know immediately. Then one day, Omble met his teacher in the busy marketplace in Medha. 'He laid down prostrate. I told him it's a crowded market, but that is the kind of respect he had for me,' says Mhaskar. Often, when he returned to the village, Omble would keep Mhaskar abreast about his family, his daughters' education, their marriage and mundane events in his life.

Mhaskar remembers the day he stood next to Omble's bust installed by the state government at Girgaum Chowpatty in Mumbai. 'I was visiting my son. And all of us decided to go to Chowpatty one evening. I saw his statue and I was overcome with emotion. But I also felt proud, and I had to take a picture that day,' Mhaskar says, showing the photograph on his phone, in which he is seen next to the bronze bust in his white kurta pyjama. 'He was an ordinary man who did something extraordinary,' Mhaskar said.

Mhaskar Guruji says that he lived his most memorable day as a schoolteacher on 17 January 2010, which would have been Omble's fifty-fifth birthday. That was the day the Plague Baba temple was inaugurated and, he says, at least 70 per cent of Omble's school classmates were present at the inauguration. A few steps away from the temple is the school where Mhaskar once taught Omble.

'Forty years after I taught them, they gathered in the same classroom that they once sat in wearing their half-pants. And just like it was those many years ago, they all sat down on the floor, they asked me to sit on the chair. I told them they were all beyond my teaching now but I would like to hear what each of them was doing. They told me, one by one. And everyone in that class felt the absence of

Tukaram,' says Mhaskar. 'Very few are lucky to experience such a day.'

* * *

The Worli sea face has a busy promenade on most evenings. Joggers, walkers, couples, groups of friends and families all take a few moments watching the waves rise and splash against the rocks. Since 2008, the Bandra-Worli Sea Link has been an additional draw for tourists and motorists alike. A hop-skip-and-jump from the promenade are the police quarters, still the residence of the Omble family. And yet, for all the years they spent in Worli, the Ombles never went to the sea face as a family. 'We just never did,' says Vaishali.

Since he was martyred, the chowk on the Sir Pochkhanawala Road, home to plush residences, including those of politicians, police officers and bureaucrats, bears the name of Tukaram Omble. He spent much of his life in Mumbai in the humble police quarters on the same road.

In the Omble household, however, nothing was the same after 26 November 2008. 'We don't celebrate any festivals. We can't do it without him,' says Vaishali.

Diwali used to be a busy affair with the patriarch taking the lead, his daughter says. It was he who picked the kandeel (lantern) every year. 'That year he had bought one lantern for Diwali. But then he bought another one because, he said, he liked it when he saw it at the market.

We now wonder if at some level he wondered who would buy one for the next year,' Vaishali says.

Rangoli patterns outside the house would be made by the Omble sisters under their father's supervision. 'He would suggest what colours to use. He always took interest in everything we did,' she says.

In the ten years that he has been gone, Omble's wife and daughters have tried to keep things just as he left them. Among the memories they preserved are not just the lantern he bought. 'We have kept everything from his uniform and clothes to his shoes. It makes us feel as if he is still with us. He was a very good carom player. We have kept the carom board because it has his touch. No one really plays with it much, except when my elder sister's children visit. But we have kept it just the way it was,' says Vaishali.

Also carefully preserved is a portrait of a couple bearing a striking resemblance to nineteenth century social reformers Mahatma Jyotirao Phule and his wife Savitribai Phule. Easily mistaken for the advocates of women's education and upliftment of Dalits, Vaishali explains that the painting is in fact that of her grandparents Gopal and Shevanta Omble.

'My father was once rewarded for nabbing an accused in a case,' she says. He used the reward money to get the portrait of his parents made by a local artist.

Omble was awarded the Ashok Chakra posthumously. His death in his uniform was as heroic as it was devastating for his family. Since his death, they have had many visitors. Apart from his colleagues, friends, family members there has been a string of politicians, reporters and families of other martyrs. Every year on 26/11, there is a flurry of calls from television news channels and newspapers. Vaishali has mostly been doing the talking for the family. The rest of them decided to stay away.

With four daughters, Vaishali says, Omble wanted them to have all the skills and training they needed to be independent. 'He did not like it when people talked about him not having a son. He took great pride in his daughters and he wanted us to learn as much as we could. When we studied at night, he would stay up with us. He would bring us coffee and just be around making sure we had everything we needed,' says Vaishali.

'He loved children but he loved daughters more. He always felt that daughters, not only his own but everyone's everyone else's daughters needed to be loved and supported all the way. He may have been stern with young boys sometimes but he would do everything in his capacity to keep little girls happy, giving them the encouragement they need,' Sulabai remembers.

Vaishali remembers a cousin's wedding in Kedambe. 'For some reason we couldn't get anyone to etch mehendi designs on her palms. It meant so much to my father. He asked how the bride could not have mehendi on her palms at her wedding. But as there was no one, he bought a mehendi cone and made the designs himself,' she remembers vividly.

To say that he was a doting father, in Vaishali's view, would be an understatement. His bond with his daughters was almost telepathic. He could almost read their minds and their wish was, unfalteringly, his command. 'One summer when we were in our village, I spotted a ripe mango on a high branch of a mango tree. I had my heart set on it and just for that reason, my father scaled the tree and plucked that mango for me. He could do that at the age of fifty-three,' Vaishali says.

At home, Omble was a family man through and through. He never brought work home. And on his days off, on many occasions, he took control of the kitchen. His culinary skills, his family in Worli and Kedambe agree, were enviable. He had his specialties and his family savoured them.

Among his favourites were pav-bhaji, a staple on the streets of Mumbai and chicken biryani that he made for his daughters from scratch. His cousin Shankar says, 'Whenever we would visit him in Mumbai, he would cook mutton for us all by himself. He was a very good cook.'

Sulabai has another memory. 'When we were young he taught me to make a dosa. I didn't know how to make it and every time I tried it would come out wrong. Then he said to me, *aga, tu yedi ka khuli* (are you mad or are you crazy)? Then he started making them and they all came out just perfect.' She allows herself a mischievous grin. 'I told him to keep making more so I could learn from him. And as he kept making them his brother and I kept eating.'

One of his favourite dishes was palak paneer. And when he wanted Tarabai to cook that for him, he would always buy the necessary ingredients a day ahead. On 25 November 2008, he asked Tarabai to buy the leafy vegetable, the chillies, garlic and other ingredients. On his way back home from work he bought the paneer. He wanted his family to have it the next day.

Omble had lived to see his two elder daughters get married. Vaishali and her younger sister Bharti were still students when he passed away. Bharti is now posted as an assistant commissioner in the sales tax department, a government job she secured on compassionate grounds. Vaishali completed her M Ed and coaches school students in the home daily. They never imagined life after their father to be easy. But the Mumbai Police department has always been there for them.

Vaishali feels grateful for the support of the police department, every police commissioner since and the late Maharashtra Home Minister R.R. Patil who they had direct access to and always found prompt help in. Karkare kaki, as she refers to Kavita Karkare, the late wife of former Maharashtra ATS chief Hemant Karkare, also martyred on 26/11, had also been a hand to turn to in times of need. Her passing away in 2014 also deepened a wound that the family nursed over the years.

'We had that one thing in common. We were families of martyrs. We would talk to each other. She would check on us from time to time. I would accompany her to places. We always reached out to her for help. She was always there for us,' Vaishali remembers fondly. She says that while they have been fortunate to have the support of many, her heart aches for families of martyrs made to run from pillar to post for what they should be rightfully given by governments.

'In Satara district alone there are so many families of martyrs. They reach out to us for help. We help in whatever way we can. But this is not how martyrs' families should be treated. They deserve more respect than that,' says Vaishali.

Nearly ten years after their loss, Tarabai and her two daughters are bracing themselves for perhaps the biggest change of their lives. They have bought a new flat in Thane and by the end of the year they hope to move there. The flat, roomier than the police quarters, may help Vaishali increase the capacity of her coaching classes. But the women can feel the burden on their chests. The breeze from the sea face, the dust from the neighbouring flour mill, the close-knit circle of neighbours have all been receptacles of childhood memories, their struggles, their triumphs and of the man who was once at the centre of it all.

They have been trying to muster the strength to take the big step. Perhaps, they say, they may achieve it by the end of the year. For now, the decision is on hold. '*Paay nighat nahi* (can't set a foot out),' says Vaishali.

Chittaprosad, *Untitled*, brush and ink on paper, 1944
Collection: DAG

4

Surviving an Execution

Kavitha Iyer

For Apurva Parikh, it all began a few weeks before 26/11 with a whiff from an incense stick, the flicker of a lamp and a statue of Shiva, a snake coiled around his neck. 'To light an agarbatti and do a quick aarti before leaving for work is a childhood habit,' he recalls. 'A few weeks before 26/11, I noticed a new figurine of Shivji in my pooja room. I complained silently when I saw it. What was the need for one more idol?' I asked.

'And over the next few weeks, on a couple of occasions, I experienced this strange sensation—a vision of Shivji's cobra wrapping itself around my neck and choking me, its flared hood by my face. I think it was happening because I was disrespecting the idol.'

The sensation, fleeting as it was, stayed etched so deep in his mind that even as he stared at death on the night of

26 November 2008, the image returned. 'When we were lined up along a staircase and the terrorists began shooting at us, I turned to my side, bracing for the bullet. Just as I fell against the wall, Shivji's snake came back coiling itself around my neck. This was it, I thought. That's when the snake's face appeared next to mine, making me move my face a few inches. And just then, the bullet whizzed past my face, ever so slightly grazing my neck.'

Apurva, sixty-seven, is visibly disturbed as he recalls the incident for the first time in nine years. But this memory is what he has armed himself with, this curious blend of faith and belief, of the physical and the metaphysical, to live life after a near-death experience on 26/11.

As one of only four men who survived an execution in a line-up of hostages inside the Hotel Oberoi on the night of 26 November 2008, his account of the night might have been one of indisputable grit and nerve. But while every anniversary of the attacks is an acknowledgement of the second chance life gifted him, the day also comes as a reminder that he survived while two of his closest friends didn't.

'I felt guilty,' he says of the most overpowering emotion he felt in the days immediately after his rescue. Over time and having laboured hard to find a deeper balance, Apurva has overcome much of the darkness he felt through December 2008. But he still can't face the wife of one friend who died, and the passage of time could not reverse the souring of ties. 'Friends and family don't say it, but I can feel it,' he says of the burden he still carries. It hurts less now, but the pain is a lasting one.

Ten years later, there is only one detail about his ordeal that's fuzzy in his memory: He doesn't know exactly why, or how, he ducked when a fusillade of bullets from two AK-47 machine guns claimed about fifteen others who'd been made to stand in a row with him, including his two best friends.

Everything else, even all these years later, is a crystal-clear recollection.

* * *

It was not just another weeknight meet-up with friends. Apurva had invited his two closest friends to discuss a deeply personal matter—his will. They'd picked Kandahar, the Indian restaurant on the first floor of the Oberoi Hotel, barely a kilometre down the road from his home on Marine Drive. His friends lived farther away and they picked him up. As they drove past the Marine Plaza, another star hotel on Marine Drive with lavish views of the Arabian Sea and Mumbai's famed Queen's Necklace, Apurva wondered for the briefest moments if pizza at Geoffrey's there might not be a better option. He didn't voice the thought, however, for they had a reservation at the Kandahar, and soon they were being ushered to their table. Around 10 p.m., they had not even placed their order when gunshots rang out downstairs. 'We knew immediately that something was seriously wrong.'

The staff at the Kandahar could see from the mezzanine the mayhem wreaked within minutes at the ground floor restaurant The Tiffin, and tried to herd the diners out quickly into the kitchen and out from a back exit. The heavy kitchen door was bolted shut even as one gunman came rushing up. Bursts of machine gunfire close behind them, Apurva and his friends joined a small crowd of diners stumbling down a stairway leading out from the kitchen's fire exit when a second terrorist emerged from below. They were trapped.

It appeared that the two terrorists had sketchy instructions to take hostages. The trapped diners, shaking and crying, were huddled together when somebody's phone rang. One gunman barked at them to throw their cell phones away. Eventually, about twenty of them, of various nationalities, were marched up the service stairway to the eighteenth floor. Apurva remembers a foreign Muslim couple saying prayers in Arabic—they were allowed to go. He also saw a couple of others slip out from the doors on the landings—he tried too, but found one locked and later the opportunity to slip out unnoticed didn't present itself. Meanwhile, smoke from grenades and a fire from a lower floor began to fill the stairwell. Coughing, breathless and some of them crying, they made it to the landing of the eighteenth floor where the hostages were lined up against the wall. One gunman was speaking on a cellphone, apparently to a handler. Execute the hostages, was the instruction. The gunmen took their positions on the upper and lower landings of the flight of stairs, and opened fire simultaneously.

'I was sure then that it was all over,' Apurva says. It is evident that even a decade later, the memory torments him.

He recounts the events of the night slowly, in a voice so low it is almost inaudible at times. Describing the massacre on the stairwell, there are long, silent pauses as he battles waves of emotion, but each time he gathers himself and continues softly.

He was near the centre, his friends were on either side of him. He ducked and turned his face almost 180 degrees, his neck at a full stretch. He felt the bullet graze his neck—had he not turned that far back, it would have hit him in the throat. He fell, bodies around and on top of him. One more spray of bullets was aimed at the heap of bodies. Once again a bullet hit him, this time in the back, but passed through causing only superficial damage. Two AK-47s, high muzzle-velocity guns, had shot them from close range. Blood was gushing out from his fellow hostages' injuries, slicking down his face and hands.

As the gunmen left the area, he lost track of time, it could have been minutes or much longer before he gathered the courage to move in the crush of bodies. There were three other survivors, at least one seemed to have a serious injury. They dared not emerge from the pile of corpses, moving only their fingers to check the others. His friends were both dead. He lay still for a long time, choked with emotion but also frozen in fear as the rattle of machine gunfire continued from various parts of the hotel below them. The stairway was also still filled with smoke. At one point, the gunmen returned, and appeared to film the bodies at the bloodied site of the slaughter. The four survivors held their breath, playing dead. When the gunmen left this time, Apurva and the three others decided it was too dangerous to stay there. Communicating only by gesticulating, the terrorists not far below them, they decided to walk up the stairway to the very top. There, they found themselves facing what appeared to be a room housing the heating and air-conditioning systems of the hotel.

The four of them would spend the next two nights hiding in the room, relieving themselves in a corner and surviving on sips of filthy water from the air-conditioning unit until the attack at the Oberoi wound down and an NSG team evacuated them on Friday morning.

'Over time, I made my peace with what happened. The memories remain, they will never go away, but as time passes they trouble me less,' Apurva says.

* * *

By the time Rohan Parikh returned to Mumbai from France where he was completing his MBA, the city would never be the same.

Apurva's eldest son, now thirty-nine, remembers being struck by the hush in Mumbai when he landed, and the complete unpreparedness of those responsible for the city's security. He took an eight-hour flight into Mumbai and arrived on the afternoon of Friday, 28 November, after spending a day anxiously waiting in his Fontainebleau residence for the attack to end. He'd had an uneasy flight, despite the airline staff trying their best to give him privacy and making sure he was the first one out of the aircraft. Rohan and his girlfriend, now his wife, had no checked-in baggage to wait for and were out of the Chhatrapati Shivaji International Airport in less than ten minutes and in a car homeward.

'The most surreal sign was getting off the plane in Mumbai. There wasn't a policeman or soldier in sight at the airport,' he remembers. On a working day afternoon, they drove down a deserted highway with no idea if the danger had been neutralized or if the roads were safe.

The next day was spent attending to his father, and accompanying the family to funerals. In the wee hours of the following day, Rohan sat down to compose an email, one that would go viral in subsequent weeks, shared by thousands of groups and message boards. He addressed it to teachers and classmates at INSEAD, to say he'd return to complete his course but after a short leave of absence. But his message, feeling his dad's pain and that of his siblings, and no doubt mirroring the thoughts of hundreds of Mumbai families that week, resonated among millions. He wrote of how the terrorists had attacked at every level, killing workers, diners in luxury restaurants, tourists, and people of multiple nationalities in a systematic slaughter.

'We have lost a lot of friends, colleagues, and acquaintances. Every person who lives in South Mumbai has a story about how either they or someone they love either died or had a narrow escape. The true extent of the horror will only make itself clear over the next few days. Mumbai is a proud city and we pride ourselves on bouncing back from any adversity. We survive and prosper despite all the difficulties placed on us. We are no strangers to terror and have had to pick up the pieces and move on after several attacks. This time, however, the sheer scale and audacity brought the city to its knees. The openness of our society, the bustling hoards (sic) in our train stations, the vibrancy of our news media, and the thousands of tourists, diplomats, and business leaders packing our hotels was used against us to devastating effect,' he wrote, agonizing over how to fight such hate, 'inject humanity into such monstrosity' and somehow maintain our values in the face of cold-bloodedness.

'Over the next week as we say goodbye to those we lost and help those that survive, Mumbai and India will ask themselves these questions. I hope the rest of the world does too,' his email said.

A couple of years later, Rohan made a conscious choice that he would get married at the Taj. Ask Apurva about it and he says it was the kids' choice of venue, he just went along with it. But Rohan saw it as an opportunity to take a stand. 'It was definitely not easy planning the wedding at the Taj. But we had a very important reason to make that choice. We decided specifically to host the event at the Taj and no other place, because we wanted it to be a message that we, like our city, were resilient and that we wouldn't be frightened. It was also a way to stand up for the city and for what happened,' Rohan says.

The experience served to alter Rohan's politics a great deal, a loss of innocence for him in a way.

'I was extremely liberal in my outlook, in terms of foreign policy I was a dove in many ways.' The attacks of 26/11 and the details that emerged from the subsequent investigation led him to feel that there is a danger to Indian democracy and society from powers keen on dividing Indians citizens. 'On the one hand we must never lose sense of our humanity, but on the other side we must never let our defences down. I support a strong Indian military, our nuclear programme, what Prime Minister Modi did in the retaliatory attacks across the border in Kashmir. I think that if we present a soft target we will become one,' he says now.

But Rohan returns often to thoughts he has expressed repeatedly since his email of November 2008, that the real question remains how to stay strong and make the enemy fear us while still keeping intact our ideals, our sense of freedom, inclusion and identity.

In 2016, he would write in an article published on *The Indian Express* website: 'How do we convince those who think they kill in god's name that no God would condone such barbarity? How do we maintain our own values and humanity when faced with such hate and provocation? . . .'

* * *

In the microseconds between the gunmen's signal to each other and the rain of bullets, Apurva says he visualized an image of his entire life till then, formed by 'flashbacks coming so fast' that he could see his parents, brother, sister, his wife, children, his businesses all in that single moment. He saw also the incomplete things—the first one was that his two sons and daughter were not ready yet to don the mantle at work.

When Apurva's father Natvarlal came to Mumbai from Ahmedabad, the city was at the cusp of a new era of industry amidst ebbing colonial rule. In 1947, he set up his first enterprises in the logistics sector, starting with government contracts, including with the Food Corporation of India, before diversifying into container transportation, freight forwarding, port management, cranes and more. He'd also purchased large tracts of land in the Chembur area, then a newly added part of Bombay City, an industrial quarter on a former swamp land.

The family lived in Sikka Nagar in Girgaum in those days, and one of Apurva's earliest memories is of being sent off to the Lawrence School, Sanawar, when he was just a primary schoolboy, his mother sobbing as he boarded a Bombay-Chandigarh train, especially booked for Sanawar-bound students from the city. His father was quite the disciplinarian, he remembers, something that he tweaked in his own parenting style to retain only as non-negotiable insistence that his kids work hard at school and arm themselves with a sound education.

Back in Mumbai to complete his higher studies at Jai Hind College, a teenaged Apurva would accompany his father during any spare time to government auctions, or would look after their workshop. Joining the business was a natural decision when he finished college and, along with his brother, he began to expand the business, taking up shipping and freight, also establishing a freight station in Deonar. It was then, nearly two decades ago, that they also thought of developing their large parcel of land in Chembur into the Acres Club. Ambitious by nature, he was keen from early on to expand on the base they had inherited. 'I was taught from a young age not to put all my eggs in one basket.'

Of his father, Apurva says, 'He was a strong-minded person. He never believed in defeat.' If he inherited his father's determination, he also took after his mother's spiritual inclinations. Though he is a Vaishnav and his wife Neela a Jain, his faith embraces Tirupati Balaji, Siddhivinayak, Shirdi Sai Baba and the Mahalaxmi goddess. At one point, when he was younger, he would visit three Mumbai deities every Sunday. Surviving 26/11 with only minor injuries deepened his belief. 'I have asked why, why me, why them—these thoughts don't go away,' he says.

He also took up yoga, the pranayam and exercises helping calm his mind and energizing it positively. Eight or nine years of yoga with a tutor has brought him a certain mindfulness that he relishes.

The big change over the years since the attack, however, is that he has become quieter, more introspective, casting away anger and impulsive bouts of ill temper. 'My nature changed all of a sudden, though it is only now after so many years that I realize what actually happened,' he says.

While being held hostage and later while hiding with the other survivors, his mind had run through the many responsibilities he still had—he and his friends had not even begun discussing his will, Rohan was still completing his MBA, younger son Romil had only just begun taking an interest in the business, daughter Anuja was in university in Chicago. He thought about his children's weddings, their future. 'How far back I was lagging in things to be done,' he thought. But as months passed later, he let things run their natural course, not speeding anything up. 'The main goal was to bring the children into the business and let them run it further.' Today, the Apurva Natvar Parikh Group's businesses span shipping, logistics, a school, a club and a hotel, the last two being more recent additions. The younger Parikhs want to expand the hotel business, Apurva says proudly.

* * *

Others in the family had to learn to cope too. Romil, now thirty-six, recollects the first few hours being just 'jacked on adrenalin' as he stood outside the Oberoi. His mum was in Pune and rushing back, Rohan in France and Anuja in Chicago, and they were calling him repeatedly in the hope of some information; his grandmother was waiting anxiously at home; he was trying to call senior police and government officials they were acquainted with who may offer a glimmer of hope. Around that time, the two gunmen, who had hijacked a police vehicle from Cama Hospital a few kilometres away, were ordering the owner of a Skoda car out of his vehicle near Vidhan Bhavan, not far from the Air India building at Nariman Point where Romil and dozens of other worried families were waiting. He heard shots fired from very close. It was well past midnight. 'We dived into the hedge outside Air India Building. A very old couple whose daughter-in-law was inside the Oberoi was also there with us. I eventually decided it was time to go home, and convinced them to leave too.' A thoroughbred Mumbaikar, Romil could not recognize what the city had suddenly turned into, deserted streets feeling like a war zone. A few hours later, when he returned to his vigil outside the Oberoi around daybreak on 27 November, the police had set up a cordon, the media had gathered, his phone was still ringing off the hook as worried friends and relatives called to check in, and there was still no news of Apurva.

He saw the best and worst of the city. His only meal for hours was a cup of tea and a snack handed out by somebody outside the Air India building. Even as he felt disappointment at the aggressive media coverage, he saw something else. 'The people of the city had banded together.' At one point, he was directed to a man who had just emerged from the Oberoi and was sitting inside the nearby mall. 'He had his head in his hands. He was severely traumatized. And he said nobody in there was alive, everybody was dead. That's when it hit me that we should start preparing for the worst,' he says.

It would be another night before a flood of relief washed over him when his mother called to say Apurva had been rescued. He had managed to call her. By the time he saw his dad at Breach Candy Hospital, it was noon on Friday. But very close friends' tragedies were still unfolding. He headed for their homes straight from the hospital. Rohan would arrive shortly too. On Sunday, a friend who had been dining at the Wasabi in the Taj on the 26th and had a close shave came to meet him. The two relaxed a little, even laughed about their luck, it seemed almost as if he had recovered from the stress of the last three days. 'Then I had an argument with my brother, it got very heated. Something got triggered in me and I just broke down, and cried for two hours non-stop,' he says.

Romil felt PTSD symptoms too, for days, triggered by loud sounds or press coverage of the attacks. Those three days changed him in many ways. 'It puts your life in perspective. Death can be quick, your world can be turned upside down in a matter of minutes. Other families had not made it through, there was tremendous survivor's guilt. But after a point, you make the best of it.'

The worst was over for the Parikhs, there was relief, but also deep grief. 'Dad had lost two very close friends. Not just dad, but we were all very close to them too,' says Rohan. The first week was the hardest any of them ever faced, they say.

* * *

Over the last ten years, the family has rallied around, making sure in the early days that Apurva was not reading or watching the news about the attack or the investigation. For the first six to seven years, they also accompanied him when he went back to the Oberoi's service stairway on the 26th of November, lighting candles with him to honour the memory of his slain friends. But the pilgrimage back was only scratching at a delicate scab, and they eventually began to coax him to do something different on the anniversary of the attacks, once even planning a trip out of town around the time. For Rohan, Romil and Anuja, it has been complex trying to honour the memory of two people they were very close to while also helping dad move on. It's something they're still figuring out, according to Rohan.

Apurva and Rohan both say the family has grown sensitive of risk in any situation, many of them involuntarily looking for the exits every time they walk into a restaurant. Anywhere in the world, Rohan finds it difficult to enter a hotel without gaming a terrorist situation in his mind and figuring out where he will take his family to hide in the eventuality of something untoward. 'I started learning martial arts. I decided if I ever am faced with such a situation I'm going to go down fighting,' he says.

Apurva is also in touch with the three other survivors who shared his ordeal in that HVAC room of the Oberoi. An unspoken empathy binds them, but on the occasions that they meet or talk on the phone, conversation is strictly idle banter or shoptalk. They first got together in 2010 when Apurva invited them to Rohan's wedding, but on that occasion and at all other meetings since, there is no discussion of the attack.

The experience of the last ten years has shown the family that those who survived the attacks after a very close shave, those who nearly lost their lives, need acknowledgement that what they went through was horrific, a sense that the city understands their very unique pain.

The family has also found that the passage of time has only served to sharpen the sense among many that the cause of justice must be served, not as a one-time tokenism but as a continuing commitment to citizen's interests. Rohan, for example, remembers having a rather heated conversation not so long ago with friends about the Pakistani cricket team being unwelcome on Indian cricket grounds. For somebody who not only has university friends from Pakistan but whose close Pakistani friend also sat at the table of honour at his wedding, Rohan still says in no uncertain terms that a national sporting side is to be seen as representing a country and its government. And with the Pakistan government having demonstrated its disinclination to punish the perpetrators of the 26/11 attack, he says it would be 'hard for many to swallow, especially those who suffered that day' that a game of cricket can just go on like before, unmindful of the hundreds suffering a long wait for closure. And this is so despite many survivors, including Apurva, feeling no hate but almost understanding for the ten gunmen. 'Many, including Dad, who saw the attackers up front said they were just kids and had no idea what they were doing. So I think with due respect they want to know that they are being stood by, that there is some sense that justice will prevail. Maybe that's important as closure,' says Rohan. Some things that happened soon after disgusted them too, Rohan says, including the visit of a Bollywood director to one of the sites of the attack, along with the then chief minister. He simply could never vote for the Congress party later.

All of them found that Mumbai, having encountered terror on multiple occasions earlier, had a way of emerging resilient each time. Rohan says, 'A week later it was less scary, and then a little less, and less. But there is always this kind of hole in your heart when you think of what happened. That hasn't left me till today. A feeling of anger that never leaves you—a dull anger deep inside that throbs each time you think about the senseless loss. But it also strengthens you in a way—it makes you appreciate our city, our strength and resilience. It makes you appreciate that no matter what, we'll come together, pick up the pieces and move on.'

Anuja, who spent those harrowing days of November 2008 thousands of miles away, says the event shook not just her but also everybody else she knew in Mumbai. Her friends and acquaintances across the world tried to stay in touch to fathom what was happening. 'It doesn't matter which part of the world you're in. If something like this is happening to your city, you talk about it,' she says. A decade later, she still marvels at her father's calmness through the ordeal, and also at Romil's ability to parry hundreds of phone calls and messages from agitated relatives while waiting outside the Oberoi.

Romil believes enough time has passed since the attack. 'It's time to put it to bed.' In his view those who understand what was lost also know that what was preserved is beautiful and amazing. As memories move to the back of the mind even if they don't ever fade, many things change. As Rohan says, '. . . . small parts remain and the rest go back to normal. But it remains one of the things that shape you. The impact is still there ten years later. It's hard to quantify, but it's part of our personality now.'

Chittaprosad, *Untitled*, brush and ink on paper, 1944
Collection: DAG

5

Lives on Track

Neha Kulkarni

In their one-room residence on the first floor of a suburban Mumbai slum, amid the daily humdrum of chores, Savitri Gupta, forty-five, and her two daughters try to make the best of the little time they have together during the day. Anjali, now sixteen, is busy with college and coaching classes, with plans to take entrance exams for a degree in engineering, while her baby sister Nikita, ten, is trying to make time for homework, play and catching up with mum. The mood in their little home in Sai Nagar Chawl is distinctly upbeat, even if Savitri is exhausted.

When her husband Vinod died after being shot by terrorists at the Chhatrapati Shivaji Terminus on 26 November 2008, Savitri had not imagined that this easy joy of time spent with her daughters would ever be possible. In fact, the pressing financial distress of that time, when

Vinod struggled to keep the family afloat on his earnings as a garage mechanic, is now dissipating.

When Savitri accepted a Group D category job with the Railways in the aftermath of the attacks, it was because there was no choice. A Group D job meant menial work. But having not completed even Class X, Savitri was unlikely to find formal employment anywhere. So with great trepidation she started, in 2009, as a subordinate *khalasi* or manual labourer in the mechanical department of Central Railway's Kurla diesel-shed. 'Pulling engines, fixing the old ones, basically doing labour-intensive tasks was my entire day's routine in those days. I had no house of my own nor decent savings and no helping hand to fall back on,' Savitri remembers. She had to move into her mother's home so that there were relatives to keep an eye on her daughters when she went to work. 'I found pleasure in doing my work well,' she says. A decade later, things are looking up, she agrees. She has a secure job and has already bagged one promotion with another one just around the corner.

The crowded railway station in South Mumbai, now renamed Chhatrapati Shivaji Maharaj Terminus (CSMT), witnessed the bloodiest massacre on the night the attack began, with fifty-two dead in the concourse of the terminus within minutes. Over the course of the next few weeks, the Indian Railways, one of the country's largest public-sector employers, reached out to the kin of those who had lost their lives at the railway station, offering to employ one member from each family.

The job offers were extended on compassionate grounds. Earlier, the Western Railway had offered jobs to the kin of seventy-four victims of the serial bombings of suburban local trains in July 2006. Onima Korda, deputy chief personnel officer with the Central Railway, remembers the swiftness with which the process took place after the attacks. 'The railway board made the decision to offer jobs to a single family member of every passenger who died at the station. According to rules, the husband or wife of the deceased passenger is offered the job first, and if a spouse is not available or cannot take the job then another immediate family member,' Korda says. All job offers were for the Group D category.

Official paperwork was readied within days. Mahavir Singh, who was then director with the Railway Board, wrote to the then general manager of the Central Railway's Mumbai division, permitting the appointment of 'next of kin of persons who died in the terrorist attacks'. The letter said applications would be scrutinized individually to gauge the dependence of the applicant on the deceased person.

As for all appointments on compassionate grounds, rules were relaxed so that educational qualification or age would not hinder applicants' chances. Among the fifty-two casualties at the railway terminus, job offers were made to forty-six families that were found eligible. The Railways verified the details of each and then dispatched a welfare officer to personally approach each family with the job offer.

Two cases from among the fifty-two could not be traced at all, as no records of their families were available. In two other cases, the families declined the Group D jobs. A few cases were ineligible as they had been offered other government jobs. 'There was also one case in which the father of a victim approached us seeking a job but later could not establish his relationship with the passenger,' Korda says. Eventually, thirty-four appointments were made. In some cases, family members could not accept the job offers immediately as there were health or age constraints, or other family problems.

Some of these families were in need of urgent financial aid, and the Railways cut through the usual bureaucratic processes. They approached each family with the required papers within a month. As early as January 2009, at least nineteen members of families thrown into chaos by the terror attack at the railway terminus had received offer letters from Central Railway.

They joined as khalasis, assistant pointsmen, parcel porters, cleaning staff, office peons and gangmen. The Central Railway tried to offer jobs at locations preferred by the candidate. A decade later, ten such employees continue to work in the Mumbai division, while others are spread across the East, Central, Northern and Southern zones of the railway. The Railways had hardly planned it so, but many of these are women who would have never imagined earning a salary. A handful of these women put themselves through night school and matriculation exams in order to access avenues of growth within the government employment.

Savitri, for example, is now trying to complete Class XII in order to try and slowly inch her way up the ladder. Keen to qualify for a departmental promotion, she completed her matriculation by attending classes at a night school. Recalling what it was like to teach her mother, Anjali says, 'Mum is a quicker learner than I am. She solved mathematics, spoke English and remembered history lessons as easily as a child can. She had only studied till Class VII earlier. Now she's completed her education till Class XI.'

Anjali makes it sound easy, but Savitri remembers being nervous and uncertain. Qualifying for a departmental test meant competing with a thousand other eligible candidates. She failed the departmental exams three times before finally being promoted in 2017 as a diesel mechanic. That is not the end of her road, she says, determined to grow some more.

'I have worked as a cleaner, worked with heavy tools and machines in my shed. Once, a kind senior section engineer praised my performance asking me if I had been a sportswoman. He could not believe that I could paint a coach, open its screws and then also put it all back in no time with such ease. Such compliments encouraged me to live life,' she smiles.

* * *

Ten years ago, as Mumbai picked up the pieces in the days after the terror attack, 'Baby Sheetal' received an outpouring of support. At three months, she was the youngest survivor in government-run JJ Hospital, nurses in the pediatric ward fussing over the infant as her mother recovered from a bullet injury. The family was waiting to board a train to Varanasi when terror struck at the train station in South Mumbai, and among the fifty-eight dead was Upendra Yadav, Sheetal's father.

Now ten years old, Sheetal is a shy child doted upon by her mother Sunita's cousins, nieces, aunts, and even the landlady. Sunita, thirty-one, remarried later and now has a second child, one-year-old Adarsh. Sunita is among those who took a Group D job with the Railways and is now employed at the divisional railway manager's office in Varanasi.

In her two-room rented accommodation near the Varanasi Cantonment railway station, Sunita says she remembers the events of that night in perfect detail, and also the subsequent disputes within the family over the monetary compensation she received. The job has promised her more than security, it's a chance to educate Sheetal and make sure the little girl makes something of her life.

Sunita's story is almost mirrored by that of Meera Sahani, a mother of three, who lost her husband Manohar at the railway station that night. Manohar was a sand digger, waiting at the station to board a train, when tragedy struck. In a double blow, the family had to cremate an effigy; Manohar's body was erroneously handed to another family. Meera, thirty-five, works as a clerk in the divisional railway manager's office in Varanasi.

Until 26/11, she had never even stepped out of her village in Ballia district of Uttar Pradesh, so taking the decision to take up the Railways' job offer and move to Varanasi was a leap of faith. Her youngest born, Neha, was then only a few months old. She was employed as an *ayah* at the railway hospital before being transferred to the DRM office. More life changes followed—she began to eat nonvegetarian food, because she needed to build her immunity if she was to work at the hospital. Perhaps most significantly, she made a friend in her colleague Guddi, whose husband Mishrilal Maurya was also among the dead at CSMT that night. Their shared grief and challenges as single parents drew them into a close bond that has lasted a decade.

'Guddi and I go to work together and our children are all like brothers and sisters. Both families go for outings together. It makes us forget the loneliness and the fact that we do not have husbands to complete our families,' Meera says.

Guddi, thirty-four, takes pride in the fact that she is the first woman in her extended family to make her own living. Her husband had been an auto-driver in Mumbai's suburbs. That night, he was dropping his sister and brother-in-law at the railway station when a bullet hit him. Like Meera and Sunita, Guddi too had an infant to look after at the time, the youngest of their three children. Had it not been for the tragedy, she says, she would have perhaps lived all her life in her village in the east Uttar Pradesh district of Deoria.

The children would have been in a village school. Instead, Guddi's three children are enrolled in a private English-medium school in Varanasi, a local charitable trust covering their tuition fees. Guddi says she not only took a big step in choosing to work, but also joined school to complete her matriculation, the minimum qualification required for the job of an ayah in the medical department of the Northeastern Railway.

'I had three children when I decided to complete my matriculation. I did not want to be under-qualified just because I landed the job as compensation,' Guddi says.

* * *

On the second floor of the division office at the CSMT building, also the headquarters of the Central Railway, Ramzan Shariff, thirty-two, is quite popular. Hidden by a tall stack of files, his desk is not easy to notice inside a tiny room in the personnel department. Posted as office superintendent to the senior divisional personnel officer, Ramzan says a government job was never his dream.

On the day of the terror attack, Ramzan and his family were preparing for a pilgrimage to Gulbarga, Karnataka, along with his grandfather Ibrahim Rahamatullah and a cousin sister. Waiting at the train station, like thousands of other passengers, the family panicked when they heard the sound of machine gunfire from the other end of the premises. Even as they tried to rush out, Ramzan and his grandfather were both hit by bullets, his grandfather succumbing to his injuries the same night.

'I was under treatment for over a month. It almost felt like a second birth to me. Why not, after all some parts of the second bullet are still lodged inside my body,' he says. It was his grandmother who suggested that he take the railway job when the offer came. No other male member from their joint family of fourteen could take up a job right then, so he agreed.

But performing Group D staffers' work was an unwelcome surprise. Ramzan tried to seek a transfer to a clerical position, but without luck. 'At the time of the attack, I had been all set to take up an accountant's job with a private firm in Riyadh. The starting salary there was Rs 35,000 per month. I had done some odd jobs before that, so this was obviously a great start to make some decent money in the future. Also, most of the elders at home have worked in the Middle East, and I was preparing to go there too when this incident changed everything,' recalls Ramzan, admitting that the biggest challenge for him was to accept the position as a peon, a Group D job.

'I tried everything I could—I approached seniors at the Railways, I took the help of a few local politicians hoping to persuade them to consider me for a clerk's job. I was a graduate in commerce, and lifting files and cleaning tables were not tasks that I had ever pictured myself doing.' Eventually, what persuaded him was his own medical condition. He had not yet completely recovered from the injuries, and going abroad might have been a little difficult with medical niggles that would cost more time and money. In February 2009, he accepted Central Railway's offer and joined.

He recalls the early years as being tough. He was required to be always on his toes and perform office chores that sometimes took a toll on his health, and on his mind. 'It felt like an insult often. I often pictured myself working at a luxurious office in Riyadh, which would have better suited my education and talent. But I tried to keep a positive attitude,' he says.

Ramzan delayed his marriage too. 'When I went to meet prospective brides, I would receive mixed responses. Some preferred me because I had a government job, while others looked down upon the fact that I was just a peon. One of my very close relatives turned down my family's proposal for his daughter claiming that my medical condition may worsen in the future. Overcoming these odds, I tried to stay positive. I then decided that I would get married only after I was promoted. I wanted my wife to feel proud of me,' he says.

He appeared for a series of departmental exams to get a promotion. His first breakthrough came in 2012 when he was promoted to junior clerk. Ramzan now has two sons.

* * *

Four hundred kilometers from Mumbai, the narrative was not very different for Amir Rampure, twenty-eight, who joined as a cleaner at the Solapur division railway hospital. His father, Aziz Rampure, who died in the attacks, shared a very good rapport with leaders of various political parties in the region. Their family had a large onion trading business. But at eighteen, Amir decided he would begin his career sweeping floors and dusting rooms in a railway office.

'I was going to take my higher secondary exams the next year. I wanted to pursue engineering and perhaps get a job with a multinational company. I'd cleared the Common Entrance Test (CET) also. All that changed when I chose to work for the Railways,' Amir says.

He remembers being mortified at the thought that somebody in Solapur might spot him sweeping floors in the hospital. 'As I worked at the hospital, the chances of running into people known to our family were always high. I would cover my face so that people would not recognize Rampure's son doing menial jobs, because our family is quite well known in Solapur. I kept telling myself that something good would eventually come of this,' he says.

Last year, Amir married Fozia, the daughter of Rafique Hatture, a former Congress corporator in Solapur. His father-in-law then wanted to help him lobby for a better post, but Amir would have none of it. From the government hospital, he was transferred a few years later as a helper in the bungalow of the divisional railway manager in Solapur. Then, in April 2018, after eight years of struggle and appearing repeatedly for departmental exams, Amir got promoted. He is now a ticket examiner (TE) at Solapur railway station.

'I completed my graduation in arts while I worked at the hospital. Though I desired to pursue science, I knew managing time for studies and practicals could become difficult along with the job,' Amir says. What kept him going was the long-term goal of a secure government job, something that he feels will benefit the family over the years.

'My father married twice, and had five children in all. When the Railways offered the job, we decided to reserve that for me and share the ex gratia sum of Rs 10 lakh with my half-brothers. It was a suitable arrangement because they were over thirty years of age then, making it unlikely that they would take a government job at the time,' he says. His own brother still too young then, and his mother having refused to take a job, the mantle fell on him to take the opportunity that presented itself and make it work for them.

While Ramzan got lucky in being promoted to junior clerk within only three years of joining, Amir had to wait eight years for his promotion. He appeared for at least two departmental exams before he qualified for a TE's post in November 2017.

'It was a long rough patch in my life. There came a time when I did not want to continue any longer, especially while being a house-help in the DRM's bungalow. I wanted to quit and join the family business of trading onions in the market yard. Things changed for good in 2017 when two great things came into my life—my promotion and my wife,' Amir grins.

Father to a son now, he's certain that he doesn't want the boy to take a government job. 'I want my son to be an engineer. I want him to fulfill my dreams and become what I could not,' he says.

Amir and Ramzan are among many families whose horizons widened since getting a job with the Railways. Former rickshaw driver Balaji Kharatmol, thirty-five, who lost his mother Sheshabai on the day of the attacks, says the job has led to better educational prospects for his children. Balaji, who lives in Kurla in suburban Mumbai, himself received minor injuries on his back where a bullet grazed him. 'I am not highly educated,' says Kharatmol, who earns nearly Rs 30,000 per month as a Group D employee. 'A year before the attacks, my father had suffered a heart attack and died. After losing both parents, it was a difficult situation for me and my four siblings. Now with a government job, I support my younger brother and my children.' He's also rented out his autorickshaw, the additional earnings a welcome supplement. Kharatmol's teenage son wants to study electronics.

Following the implementation of the Sixth Pay Commission, the basic salary of a railway employee in a Group D job ranged from Rs 5200 to Rs 20,200 per month in 2009. There was also an additional incentive of Rs 1800 per month for medical needs and recreational facilities. For Balaji, who then made about Rs 4000 to Rs 5000 a month as an auto-driver, the Railways' starting salary was life changing.

* * *

On a similar note, Wadi Bunder resident Ali Hussain Mullah, thirty-four, understood his responsibilities only after he lost elder brother Nurool Mullah on the day of the attacks. Having worked as a contract driver at government offices, Ali's world seemed to spin out of control when his family suddenly began to look at him for support. 'My brother Nurool was the *achha bacha* of the house. He would do many odd jobs to support us. After him, I was expected to take care of the house. My mother didn't want to take the job,' says Ali, who joined as an assistant pointsman at Roha station, a distant suburb of Mumbai.

In 2014, Ali was promoted as senior pointsman, but his efforts to grow continue. 'I have filled the form to qualify as a shunting master and I also aim to become a station master someday. As senior pointsman at Chembur station, the responsibility of the safe working of the Railways in this zone rests on me, among others. Two assistant pointsmen report to me and we are always available at the beck and call of the motormen,' he says.

His two sisters work as domestic help, so Ali is keenly aware of just how much dignity and stability he has in a job that promises post-retirement benefits. 'Due to my nonchalant attitude in my growing up years, I was often told by my relatives that I would never achieve anything in life. Today, juniors report to me. I may have studied in a municipal school, but my children are in English-medium schools. We have also saved the ex gratia sum received so that my mother will undertake the Hajj pilgrimage soon,' he says.

It's not always a simple journey for these survivors rehabilitated by the Railways. Savitri, for one, says life has continued to throw her the occasional curveball. Showing scars on her neck and right cheek, she says she fell down a flight of stairs in 2012, and had to undergo a surgery that cost them most of their savings. She went through the emotional and financial turmoil alone, her daughters too young to even understand, but she says it's their presence that makes her keen to take on more challenges.

'I never wanted to remarry. On holidays, my daughters and I sit on the Scooty and ride off to shopping malls or entertainment centres. We enjoy the little pleasures in life. We like to try out new restaurants or just sit at Marine Drive when it rains. I want to give my daughters a better future, make them strong so that they can face the tough world.'

A decade of having been a working woman, Savitri says, has made one thing clear. 'Now I need no man to complete my family.'

Chittaprosad, *Untitled*, linocut
Collection: DAG

6

A Crusader Is Born

Kavitha Iyer

Sarla Parekh bristles when she reads about new Jain temples built at costs of Rs 100 crore and upwards. It is a very small community, but one with immense economic power, including a very large number of Indian titans of industry and commerce. Pained that powerful groups among the community invest in constructing ostentatious places of worship, she says those with the ability to use their resources to bring about change also have a duty to do so. A Jain herself, she still feels shocked every time she reads about a community member under investigation for a white-collar crime.

Sarla, eighty-five, is often described in newspaper reports as the grieving mother who approached courts in Mumbai after losing her son and daughter-in-law in the terror attack at the Oberoi Hotel on the night of 26 November 2008. They had kissed their two daughters good night before leaving for dinner at The Tiffin, the lobby level dining space at the five-star hotel located at the southernmost tip of the iconic Marine Drive, and were perhaps among the very first casualties when the terrorists rushed in with automatic weapons.

She filed two petitions in the Bombay High Court seeking reforms in the government's preparedness and with a view to fix accountability for the loss of lives and property in the attacks. But when she discusses that transformative day and the ten years that have passed since, Sarlaben, as the silver-haired and decidedly outspoken grandmother is known to all, holds forth on neither her grief nor her petitions in the Bombay High Court. What she really wants to discuss is corruption—in religion, in public life, in institutions, in businesses. 'Those poor boys who were sent to attack Mumbai, they were just from impoverished families, brainwashed about getting into heaven by those who recruited them. Those boys were almost sold for a price. And these poor families were just caught in a power struggle between the imams and the politicians.'

When he died, Sarlaben's son Sunil, forty-five, was managing director of United Shippers, a top lighterage, stevedoring and logistics firm with operations in various ports across the western coast, in Maharashtra, Gujarat and Goa. With Sunil gone, his only sibling Sujata turned into a pillar of support for Sarlaben. The Parekhs are blue bloods who have grown further in the last two decades. Sarlaben has commitments to a range of philanthropic causes, but not one of them is religious. In fact, Sarlaben is not a non-believer. The family has had its share of spiritual explorations in the decade since the terror attack. Also, key principles of Jainism form the central spine of Sarlaben's own worldview. But she is just not comfortable with the nature of several popular practices stemming from religion. She read recently about a new temple in Rajasthan, then another one in Gujarat. 'I don't believe in this. We don't give to any religious causes. Otherwise our home is open to people working for all kinds of good projects.'

Her daughter Sujata's daughter Tarini, works with Global Development Incubator, a New York- based organization working in East Africa and the rest of the global south to partner start-ups in the social and development space. She has made it clear that she will not join the family business—she's disinclined to work in any field in India because of the commonplace corruption in everyday dealings, Sarlaben says. But notwithstanding what happened to the family over the last ten years after losing Sunil and his wife Reshma, Tarini has learnt that corruption in religion and deliberate political distortions are quotidian, in plain sight, and yet not usually contested by people. 'She gets very angry when people talk poorly of Muslims or Islam. She says it is we who created the identities of Hindu, Muslim or Dalit, and we are responsible for what we created. She really dislikes the general prejudice towards Muslims,' says Sarlaben.

If it were up to her, she would insist upon a return to every religion's most basic tenets, the embellishments deleted, in order to tackle the general moral degradation she finds so disturbing. 'Don't harm anyone; don't utter untruths; don't take what is not yours; don't accumulate,' she counts on her fingers. That last principle of Jainism, *aparigraha*, defined as non-possessiveness or temperance, a rejection of greed or avarice, is a theme that runs right through everything she does.

Ahead of this year's monsoon, keen to build a watershed management system in the sprawling lush acres around their farmhouse in Alibag's Dhokawade village, she appointed a consultant and, based on his plans, had a farm pond dug. It needed a lining to prevent water percolating, and she didn't hesitate to call the proprietor of a very large polymer manufacturing company, keen to cut costs by asking for material at cost price. 'My family gets annoyed, they worry about what people will think of me if I negotiate for things like this. But what's wrong? Every paisa saved can be used for some other good work,' she laughs. 'I am a very simple person. I don't wear jewellery, these earrings are not real diamonds. I don't believe in showing off. I also shop only when there's a discount sale.' One of her granddaughters is considering a career in marketing and branding, much to Sarlaben's chagrin. She names two international apparel brands, one French and one American. 'Some of their products are manufactured here by somebody I know. What I can buy here for Rs 300 or Rs 350 costs $12 in the US even when it's on sale. What is the margin of the company, can you imagine? A bag retails for Rs 5 lakh because it's from a certain luxury brand, I cannot make my peace with such things.'

How does the multimillionaire matriarch of a major business family reject profiteering? 'Yes, I do belong to a business family. But that does not mean that the profit motive is the only one you understand. There have to be reasonable profits.' She says the company that inspires her the most is Indian confectioner Parle, which manufactures the famous Parle-G biscuit, the largest-selling biscuit brand in the world according to a 2011 survey by market research firm Nielsen. They make a product that's credible, hugely popular but never sold at large profits, she reasons.

* * *

As a nine-year-old girl with a large playgroup of siblings and cousins, Sarla would run around Gowalia Tank in South Mumbai, a stone's throw from their home opposite Mani Bhavan on Laburnum Road, during the heady months of the Quit India movement. The kids, also swept up in the mood of the mid-1940s even if they understood little of the significance of those years, would collect autographs from visiting leaders. She remembers getting Subhas Chandra Bose's autograph.

Sarla's father had arrived in Mumbai from Limdi in Saurashtra as a twelve-year-old boy, growing to get a broker's licence at the stock exchange and a cotton brokerage before also establishing himself as a philanthropist. He had a licenced gun, a privilege reserved for only the elite Indians in the trading community. Her mother was one among six brothers and sisters and, having lost a sister, was parenting additional children alongside her own. This meant Sarla's wardrobe had a range of hand-me-downs and used toys.

'With whatever little she had, she took care of a lot of people. We had a large family around us all the time, all of us cousins in a shared bedroom.'

Her father would make donations to the freedom movement, including a press for Independence literature. She remembers seeing Mahatma Gandhi at Mani Bhavan where they would go for prayer sessions, him addressing her mother as 'Sethani'. She remembers politician and the second CM of Gujarat, Balwantrai Mehta, visiting their home. A prominent school in the locality also received a large endowment from her father.

Her mother, a very religious woman, had not had much of an education. Nevertheless, she was an early believer in equality between the sexes, and made sure her daughters had the same education as the boys in the household. For all practical purposes, Sarla grew up in a rather modern household, her brother settled in the United States as early as 1946, and so was somewhat unprepared for the culture shock of her marital home where women were cloistered from male guests.

She married into a wealthy family in 1956. Her father-in-law had been a landowner on Mumbai's posh Marine Drive, and had built the Art Deco building they now live in as well as buildings on several other plots along the stretch, along with partners. In this home, women kept their head covered, and stayed out of the long passageway connecting the rest of the house to the living room where the men folk met guests. Sarla, who had every plan of pursuing a career, was a fish out of water in her early days in the Parekh

Rohan and Atharva Kamble, whose father Rajan Kamble, a staffer at the Taj, was shot in the abdomen on the night of the attack. Rajan died in hospital on 3 December 2008.

Slain policeman Tukaram Omble's cousin Shankar (middle) and niece
Sulabai at their home in his native village, Kedambe,
about 250 km from Mumbai.

In Kedambe, a picturesque village with lush views of hillsides,
every single resident remembers Assistant Police Inspector
Tukaram Omble's sacrifice.

Govind Singh Kathayat at his home.

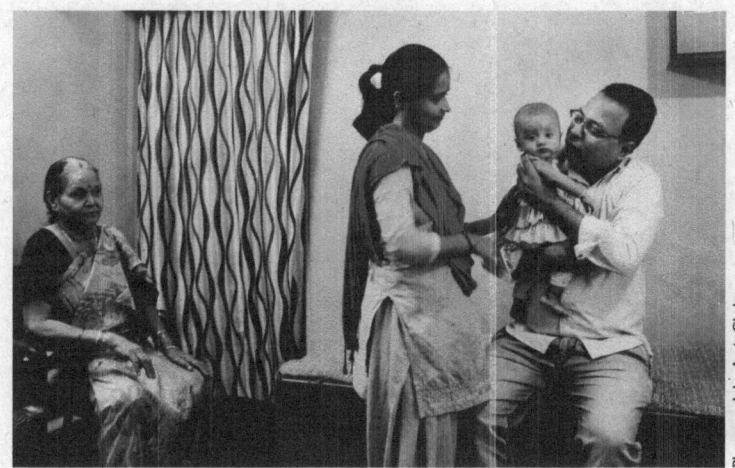

Govind Singh Kathayat with his wife, Radha, and their son, Chaitanya.
His mother, Bhagirathi, is on the left.

Devika Rotawan with her father and brother at their home in suburban Mumbai.

Kia Scherr, who lost her husband and daughter in the attack at Oberoi Hotel on 26 November 2008, in Mumbai.

Savitri Gupta at work in the Kurla diesel shed of Central Railway.

Deepak Gupta at his home in Govandi.

Sadashiv Kolake at his street-food stall in Worli.

Sevantilal and Sarla Parekh at their South Mumbai home.

Apurva Parikh (right) with his family at his residence off
Marine Drive in Mumbai.

Photograph by Janak Rathod

Photograph by Vignesh Krishnamoorthy

Dhanalakshmi and K. Unnikrishnan meet NSG commandos at *The Indian Express*'s 26/11 Stories of Strength event on 26 November 2017 at Gateway of India, Mumbai.

household. But the family had suffered losses around Independence, and her husband Sevantilal was working on a young shipping business. Seizing the opportunity, the newly married Sarla convinced her mother-in-law that her taking a job would help her network in business circles, and so in 1957 she took a job with General Insurance Co. Meanwhile, United Shippers took flight, and Sunil was born in 1963.

By 1969, Sarlaben began to be closely associated with the Kasturba Health Society, formed in the early 1960s to run a hospital in Sevagram, Wardha, where Gandhi lived for nearly eight years. It used to be a thirty-bed hospital in those days after being set up in 1945 by Sushila Nayar, a close associate of Mahatma Gandhi, especially to offer quality healthcare to rural patients. The principles of austerity and minimalism that Sarlaben espouses were a perfect match with the Kasturba Society, and she has continued to channel much of the family's charitable work towards the hospital, now a 980-bed hospital with a large government grant.

That commitment to business and social interests kept the Parekhs in India, though both Sarlaben and Sevantilal had family members who had migrated to the US. Sevantilal says he had considered moving too, but by then there were ageing parents to look after.

At eighty-five, Sarlaben still has a packed appointment calendar—her various social initiatives, caring for the farmhouse and land in Alibag, her 300 coconut trees there, personally supervising the cold-press process of extracting the coconut oil, physiotherapy sessions, yoga in the mornings, FaceTime with the granddaughters in New York.

The doting grandparents found themselves sharing parental responsibilities once again, after decades, treading unfamiliar ground this time as they negotiated an all-new teenage ecosystem just when they had hit their mid-seventies. Having lost both parents in a savage twist of fate, Anandita and Arundhati, now twenty-two and twenty, went through a rough phase that outlived the initial shock by several months. Both students then at a South Mumbai school, they were living with their grandparents. 'If we went into their room, there would be no conversation. Or they would reply in monosyllables. Or they would keep talking to friends on the phone. They were deeply affected by what had happened,' says Sarlaben, adding that there was a time when the gap between grandparents and grandchildren seemed impossible to bridge. 'The support of friends and family meant everything.' Sarlaben's daughter Sujata shouldered much of the responsibility of the girls, putting her own life on hold and taking charge of her nieces.

The girls' maternal grandmother has also tried to help fill the void. Rama Parekh, eighty, had been herself dealt a double tragedy. Only three years before the 26/11 attack, she'd lost her husband. And the terror attack took away her only child. 'Despite all the luxuries we have, look at our fate. That's karma,' says Rama, who lives alone in her Napean Sea Road flat, assisted by staff, and keeps herself busy with a Rotary Club, satsangs and a group of women she plays bridge with. 'In the initial few days I was in shock, I kept asking why I was still alive. Sarlaben was an inspiration. Then one day, Anandita said she wants *naani* around. And that's when I realized that my purpose is to be there for them. My grandkids are my world now,' she says. She likes teaching Anandita and Arundhati a little Jain philosophy whenever she can. She also makes it a point to write a handwritten note to each of them on their birthdays. 'When they were younger they'd come to visit me every weekend, and I'd teach them something—a little cooking maybe. I taught them the *Navkar* mantra when they were still quite young, it is Jainism's most important chant. All this gives me a chance to be their grandmother in a wholesome way.'

Rama also spent months compiling a book on Reshma, a coffee-table book. She printed just two copies, one placed in either grandparents' home for the girls to re-acquaint themselves, over and over, with what Reshma's friends and relatives thought of her. She trawled her late daughter's Facebook account and got in touch with friends across the world to request snatches of memories and old photographs that she then painstakingly put together as a book.

When Anandita graduated in the summer of 2018, all three grandparents made the journey to the US. As they finish their studies and make complex career choices, the girls have grown to be warm and affectionate towards all three grandparents. They also have an inclination towards social causes.

On a previous holiday back home, Anandita spent time teaching children from an orphanage to dance and then organized a charity dance show. The trustees at Bharatiya Vidya Bhavan are known to Sarlaben and so a venue was arranged quickly. 'She called all my friends and made them buy tickets, and then donated the money she collected to the orphanage.'

Sevantilal says they took a conscious decision to make all three granddaughters NRIs. 'If they choose not to return to India, we won't be unhappy,' he says. He explains that the girls have learnt to be independent in settings very different from what they'd been accustomed to, far removed from their life in Mumbai where they had never so much as seen the inside of a public transport bus or a train. Dangers lurk too commonly in Indian society now, Sarlaben feels, counting off on her fingers, 'Drugs, terror, blasts, rape. Especially those with daughters want to leave India.'

* * *

Late in 2008, when the occasion arose to participate in litigation demanding accountability from various arms of the government and private institutions for the damage caused by the attack, Sarlaben felt she didn't have a choice but to get involved.

The reason, she says now, was that despite years of social work and having been closely acquainted with the daily realities of the less fortunate, she had somehow been comfortable in the assumption that certain kinds of tragedy do not hit people like them. Until 2008, terror attacks in Mumbai had targeted tourists and working-class people at the Gateway of India, outside crowded marketplaces, or even aboard suburban local trains. Wealthy foreign tourists living in five-star hotels and equally wealthy Indians dining at luxury restaurants had been cosseted, until now. But November 2008 had reordered that equation, and she felt in her gut that it was up to those living in the city's most rarefied environs to decide whether they would get involved or let their inertia weaken public campaigns.

Retired senior bureaucrat B.G. Deshmukh and former police commissioner Julio Rebeiro had been working on governance-related issues in Mumbai for several years before they happened to meet Sarlaben, entirely by chance. Her chartered accountant was working with them on a series of Right to Information clinics they were organizing in the winter of 2008, and he happened to mention her, the mother of a young couple killed at the Oberoi on the night of 26/11. Immediately, they wanted to meet her.

Eventually, Sarlaben partnered with their Public Concern for Governance Trust to file two suits, neither of which ended favourably at the time. But she took the battle all the way to the Supreme Court, even collecting money from concerned citizens willing to fund a CCTV surveillance system for Mumbai. The courts ordered that building such infrastructure was the prerogative of the government alone. The suit was on various e-surveillance measures, mobile phone interception systems and CCTV cameras for Mumbai's streets. Preemptive security systems in Mumbai, and indeed across Indian cities, continue to lag behind the West, she laments, talking at length about technologies available to prevent similar or wildly more unimaginable attacks in the future. And technologies in use in the West are available for purchase, she says. Nothing emerged directly from that petition, but nearly ten years ago, they had already added valuable insights to the dialogue on security upgrades.

Today, Sarlaben is aware of what contribution their suit made to public discourse on the subjects of safety and policing in Mumbai. A vast CCTV network is taking shape in Mumbai, though it is a work in progress, and though it took its time coming.

The other petition was on the matter of compensation for the victims, on which the court directed them to various lower authorities first, including the five-star hotels that had been attacked, before the HC would hear it. She felt that on the matter of what the petitioners perceived as negligence by the hotel authorities, she was on solid ground, with evidence. One five-star hotel had relaxed security owing to a politician stepping in to ease the experience for visitors to a function his friend was hosting, she claims. Other five-star hotels had followed suit, despite police warnings and intelligence inputs in the past that such properties could be soft targets. 'I wasn't interested in the money. I consulted senior lawyers and they said that it could be another fifteen years before the court heard such a suit. I am eighty-five years old now, who will appear as a witness after me?'

As an additional measure, in an effort to raise consciousness and awareness on public policy, she decided that if people's moral fibre has to be rebuilt, the process must begin in childhood. That led her to initiate a memorial event on 26 November, later adding a second event on Republic Day. 'We've been doing it for ten years now. We gather students from schools and colleges for a programme, including skits and exhibitions and demonstrations, on what's ailing our security system, how corruption is gnawing away at the roots of institutions. Rebeiro gives a short lecture.' An income tax commissioner and a few other senior bureaucrats are also involved now, and Sarlaben hopes the scale of the event will grow in coming years.

Then there was the matter of dealing with the grief. Describing herself as somebody brought up with a measure of detachment, she says it was her husband who was more deeply affected by the tragedy—to date he cannot speak about Sunil and Reshma without his eyes welling up. Speaking at the Cricket Club of India in 2008 where he was then president, Sevantilal had said in a choked voice that this particular death for his only son was something he could simply not come to terms with.

As they searched for spiritual succour, somebody sent them books about the afterlife. At the friend's suggestion, they very briefly attempted to reach out to the son they yearned to hold one more time, purportedly now in another sphere. It was not something Sarlaben could find comfort in. Perhaps it is indeed possible to know the future and to know what happens to life after death, she says. 'But I don't want to know the future. What is the point of wasting your time worrying about something bad that's going to happen?' They gave up on the suggested séance, but one suggestion from that friend remains in practice in the home even a decade later. Lamps in sets of three stay lit all day in front of the dozens of photographs of Sunil and Reshma displayed lovingly around the house.

That was Sarlaben at her practical best, accepting what made some sense and what brought a modicum of solace. 'Do the best you can. God has sent you here to do something good. Do that. And if something bad happens, take it in your stride,' she says.

Meanwhile, her niece Asha Mehta took up the cause of children affected by 26/11, many having lost the sole breadwinner of the household and facing uncertainty over their education. Sarlaben donated to Mehta's NGO Ratnanidhi Charitable Trust, which continues to assist several terror victims' families with educational expenses.

She had mixed feelings about the news of the hanging of Ajmal Kasab, the sole terrorist who survived that night. On the one hand, she felt the crores spent on securing Kasab and on the trial should have instead been spent on the children of those killed in the attacks. On the other hand, the execution did not bring a sense of justice being served. 'We are taking action against those who in my opinion are only pawns on a chessboard. Nothing has been done about the king and the queen. They still operate.'

Over ten years, she has also learnt to use the Right to Information Act, the sunshine law on transparency in governance and in government. She has arranged finances for a handful of public interest litigations and takes an interest in PCGT's clinics helping citizens to use the freedom of information law, whether it is to question local government or municipal authorities, get income tax refunds or simply access data on public spending. 'Integrity is the key,' she says, explaining that she will happily help out with a good cause even if the subject is not immediately familiar.

Sevantilal says he supports all her initiatives without any question; he has a visible pride in her tirelessness. 'But some of it is futile,' he reasons. If you look at the brass tacks of what was achieved by the litigations she put her heart in, the CCTVs are now installed across Mumbai but seem to be more in use for nabbing traffic offenders more than anything else, he says. Sarlaben adds that she read a news report about an incident in Manhattan a couple of years ago where the police control room was able to stop a man reported to be carrying a suspicious bag merely through using their camera network. 'What's so technically complicated about installing CCTV networks everywhere?' she asks.

According to Sevantilal, it was a few years after 26/11 that a business associate abroad suggested that he partner in a proposed deal for suggested new equipment for Mumbai Police. A commission had been discussed, which would have rendered the deal unprofitable. Sevantilal thought he could reach out to a friend in the police force, a very senior official. He had to return shocked, somebody he had considered a close friend had more or less refused to relax the demanded 'commission'. Such payoffs are a reality nobody can escape, he had shrugged. Sevantilal says he felt a deep disgust, especially because it was a contract related to better policing.

115

If proprietors take money out of the company, and if that is condoned or swept under the carpet, the entire institution begins to accept that there is a culture of corruption that everybody must partake of, he says. 'Is this our culture?' he asks. 'I love my country and presumably there is a god who can correct this situation,' he says. 'We have only some kind of satisfaction that we are doing our best.'

Over the last decade, Sarlaben has also turned into something of a letter-writer, penning missives to officials, politicians and institutions, believing that voicing her thoughts is the first step towards trying to make a difference. She was visiting Nagpur a few years ago and met a friend who was facing difficulties in accessing her own property owing to an overstaying tenant. 'I wrote to Chief Minister Devendra Fadnavis, and congratulated him in advance for helping people like her, in contrast to previous regimes that had helped encroachments persist.' Eventually, 900 families got their homes back after authorities intervened. On another occasion, a client told her he had sold his company in order to dedicate himself to manufacturing prosthetics, but eventually found he couldn't sell them in India because he simply couldn't afford to pay the commissions. 'I wrote to Prime Minister Narendra Modi about this,' she says. 'To effect change, you have to be bold, speak out.'

Ram Kumar, *Two Sisters*, lithograph, 1958
Collection: DAG

7

The Migrants' Tale

Sadaf Modak

For several years, Shivshankar Gupta and Sadashiv Kolake worked within a kilometre of each other. Shivshankar was a *bhelpuri* vendor at the Chhatrapati Shivaji Maharaj terminus. Sadashiv worked as a kitchen staffer at a restaurant near the Crawford Market, a heritage building named after the first colonial municipal commissioner of the city of Bombay. On nights when he had no roof over his head, Sadashiv slept at the train station, not far from platform number 7 where Shivshankar walked with his basket of puffed rice, peanuts, chopped vegetables and spice powders, serving his quick-fix snack in cones fashioned from old newspapers.

As is the norm in Mumbai, the two men never met. But the terror attack on the night of 26 November 2008, drew their stories close together, their families' narratives

119

now mirroring one another's painful journey out of poverty compounded by tragedy.

Both men had dropped out of school due to poverty. Both began working from a very young age. Both struggled to make ends meet, nurturing secret hopes for their families and especially their children. Until that point, their stories were two among millions of similar accounts in the city of dreams.

But both were also at the train station that night when terrorists Ajmal Kasab and Abu Ismail opened fire. Shivshankar was one of the fifty-eight persons shot dead at the station. Sadashiv, hit by a bullet on his neck, survived.

Sadashiv was then working at the Swastik Lunch Home near Crawford Market and was only dropping off a colleague at the railway station. Having worked alone in numerous hotels since coming to Mumbai as a thirteen-year-old, his 'family' in the city were his co-workers. On that night, one of them was returning to his native village in south India and had a lot of luggage. 'We were waiting at the station for the train to arrive after 10 p.m. We heard a commotion followed by gunfire. People were running, trying to escape. My colleague and I got separated. I tried to run too, but I was hit by something and fell on the floor. There was blood all around. I do not remember who rushed me to the hospital. When I woke up, my employer was there by my side,' Sadashiv says. Policemen had used his cell phone to contact his employer who rushed to the nearby Gokuldas

Tejpal Hospital. His family, in Kolhapur district, over 400 km away, was informed. 'My wife, parents and children were shocked and kept insisting that they would come to Mumbai to see me. But I lived in the restaurant where I worked and had no way to provide my family accommodation if they came to the city. I needed my family but could not call them here. Money was also an issue, I could not even afford their travel to Mumbai,' Sadashiv says, now forty-three years old. For the next few months, even as he underwent multiple surgeries at state-run JJ Hospital, he was looked after by colleagues and his employer. It was only after he could walk on his own that Sadashiv took a bus ride home, for the six months of bed rest advised by doctors.

When the attack began, Rajkumari Gupta was at home in a suburban slum colony with her four children and parents-in-law. She had just served dinner when a neighbour came rushing to say news channels were flashing details about firing in the train station. 'We did not have a TV, so all of us went to the neighbour's house. I cannot forget the images. People were running helter-skelter. I prayed that he had found a safe spot, that he had somehow managed to hide behind something,' Rajkumari recalls. Her husband Shivshankar usually returned home by 2 a.m. When it was well past the usual hour, Rajkumari began panicking. 'The trains weren't running, so I felt maybe he slept at the station. Such was our dependence on the daily wage that I thought he might return home only the next day of work,' she says. But a phone call brought the bad news soon, and Rajkumari took her son Deepak and rushed to Gokuldas Tejpal Hospital. They identified his body, but even a decade later, do not know exactly where and how the end came for him.

* * *

Growing up in a village named Thanewadi in Maharashtra's Kolhapur district, Sadashiv's earliest memories are of a large joint family surviving on whatever they could eke out from a too-small piece of land. They grew rice, but barely enough for themselves, a subsistence-level farming that meant the boys were expected to work if the family had to escape the crushing poverty. Sadashiv dropped out of school after studying only till Class II. Barely eight years old, he went to work in the fields, helping the family on their own meagre plot of land and also earning a few rupees as a labourer on bigger farms.

Other boys in the household were working too, but there was never enough to feed everyone. As the pressure to look for other livelihood options outside the village grew, at the age of thirteen years, Sadashiv came to Mumbai. The first visit was with a relative, three decades ago. He'd never seen even a small town, much less been prepared for the big city. 'My first job was in a hotel near Crawford Market, cleaning tables and utensils. At the end of the day, I would sleep in the hotel itself. Mumbai seemed so big and fast-paced then. The days would pass quickly because I was at work for long hours, but on most nights, I felt lost and missed home acutely. I would cry myself to sleep.' Several times, he thought of returning home, but the question of how he would make a living there made him stay back. His first salary was Rs 150 per month, most of which he managed to save and send home. If he missed his mother more than usual, he would seek out a colleague who could write and pen her a letter—his village didn't have its first telephone yet in those days. In his letters, he would ask about the well-being of the family and tell his mother about his work. 'I never got a response. But I continued to send the letters anyway, to feel less lonely,' he says.

He also focused his energies on his work, never letting it become drudgery. In the early months, he would observe his colleagues closely and soon, from cleaning tables, he was promoted to cutting vegetables. For the next four years, he worked at a series of hotels in the busy marketplace and commercial hub around Crawford Market, which in those days was Mumbai's market for goods purchased in wholesale.

He didn't jump jobs out of choice. A curious reality he came to be closely acquainted with was being sacked around the time he was completing three months at any job—employers were apprehensive about giving workers any kind of welfare benefits. He would usually manage to find a job soon enough, and at the new workplace also a corner to spread out a thin sheet to sleep on at night. But there were times when he could not find a job for a few days, and during those long days he would spend daytime hours looking for work and sleep in the train station at night.

As he grew older, he learnt the tricks of the trade and also acquired enough of a street-smart savoir-faire to be able to negotiate his salary with employers and also wrangle a stable job. His keen interest in observing and learning new things also got him a job as a cook in a hotel where he worked for nearly a decade.

Back home in his village, Sadashiv's family meanwhile arranged his marriage with a relative's daughter, Rekha. As he did not have a home to stay, Rekha continued to live in his village with his family while he worked in Mumbai. He would return to his new bride in Thanewadi only for brief holidays. Ten years later, the couple had a son, Omkar, followed by a daughter, Jyoti, two years later. Then the hotel he was working at closed down, and Sadashiv once again began to look for work. After a few months of doing odd jobs, he found work at Swastik Lunch Home, a restaurant frequented by South Mumbai's working-class population. That was where he was employed in November 2008.

* * *

Rajkumari Gupta, Shivshankar's wife, does not know her exact age, but surmises she must be in her forties. In the little over two decades of their marriage, she had visited his place of work only twice, after a good deal of insisting and badgering.

Both times, she was too shy to approach him directly while he was with customers and ended up telling a stranger to go up to him and let him know that his wife was there to see him. 'He took a quick break and came to talk to me. I was taken aback when I saw how he carried the bhelpuri basket around his neck. It must have weighed at least 25 kilos. I wondered how tiring it must be for him. He also showed me how he would jump off a running train as it picked up speed. It was scary to watch, but he said he was quite used to it,' she says.

After 2008, Rajkumari never gathered the courage to visit the station again. Multiple times, she rode the train up to Masjid station, the penultimate station on the Central Railway line before CSMT. 'But I have never managed to go further. How can I see that place now, the same place where he worked, where I had gone to visit him?'

The Guptas' connection with the train station actually dates back a whole generation.

Since he was a young boy, Gupta's father, Niruah, sold roasted peanuts and chickpeas outside the General Post Office in Mumbai, just south of the magnificent Victoria Terminus. It was a good location for an itinerant hawker. Hundreds of migrants assembled everyday outside the GPO to send letters and money home. Gupta, his mother and his two siblings also lived nearby in a shanty.

But the seventies saw increased monitoring of the area by municipal authorities and the family's 'home' was demolished in an anti-encroachment drive. The family moved to Mankhurd on the far eastern tip of Mumbai, about

30 km away, seeking safety in the company of thousands of other migrant families' temporary homes. The slum colony was still sparse in those days, but more and more migrants from Uttar Pradesh arrived each year, from other parts of Mumbai and from villages in the northern states.

It also became increasingly difficult for Niruah to work without a hawker's licence, so Shivshankar also dropped out of school to help buttress the family income. He worked initially in a grocery shop, making around Rs 200 per month. When he turned nineteen, Gupta married Rajkumari, who was then sixteen years old and had studied only till primary school. Over the next few years, the couple had four children, Neelam, Dipak, Sandeep and Sheetal. Gupta tried his hand at various occupations, hoping to make a better living. 'He took a job as a security guard. There was never enough to eat. He would do double shifts to earn Rs 2800 a month. It took a toll on his health and the money barely covered our expenses,' Rajkumari recalls.

It was only a few years before 2008 that an acquaintance told Gupta about a job as a hawker at CSMT, with a fixed salary of Rs 200 per day. 'This job suited him. He got paid daily and we could save some money to pay rent and the water and electricity bills. He had hoped that he could continue to work there till the children completed their studies and found jobs.'

He would leave home around 10 a.m. and return only after the children had gone to sleep, taking the last train home every day so as to not lose out on any customers.

Rajkumari would stay awake for him to return, serve him dinner, while they spoke about work and home. 'The children have grown up in these ten years. I miss him, especially our conversations at night after he came from work. We barely had enough to eat, but we made it count together,' she says. On Sundays, Gupta would usually be home, catching up on rest. 'The children would sometimes insist on an outing. We'd look at each other, wondering what to do if they demanded a toy or something to eat. Still, he took them to Chowpatty, Gateway of India, the zoo,' she says.

The children's education was top priority for the couple, even if it meant never taking a break from work. Shivshankar and Rajkumari did not visit their native village for years, in a bid to save that money. After getting his monthly railway season ticket made, he would keep only a Rs 50 note with him, stretching that for weeks. 'Now with the children finding jobs, I keep wishing he had been alive to enjoy some of the fruit of his hard work.'

* * *

Some nights, Sadashiv still wakes up in a cold sweat, remembering that he had almost died. 'My two children were very young. My family was dependent on me. What would they have done?' he says now. As the only breadwinner, however, he could not let the trauma change the trajectory of his life. The family insisted that he look for work in the village, but he decided despite everyone's apprehensions to return to Mumbai. The disparity in earnings made it a no-brainer actually.

But his return was far from a smooth ride. The ex gratia sum from the government was spent in paying off creditors. At the hotel where he worked, he had been replaced as he'd been away for six months. Unwilling to watch somebody else lose a job so that he could get his position back, he began to work at tea stalls and various food joints. Late in 2009, he started his own venture, as a stressed food vendor, starting with only a small bench from where he sold Mumbai's most popular street food, the vada pav. Later, he altered that to serve eggs—omelets, bhurji or spiced scrambled eggs and boiled eggs.

His day now begins at 6 a.m. The bench has now extended to a small cabinet where he stores his supplies. He cleans up before the bread and eggs are delivered by a supplier, then visits the nearby market to buy tomatoes, onions, green chillies and spices. By 7 a.m., he sets his griddle on the flame, and from then on gets barely a few minutes' rest during the day. He single-handedly chops vegetables, makes the omelettes and handles the cash. The money is kept in a small steel box, though for regular customers he is always accommodating if they do not have money. 'Many who eat here are migrants like myself, some come from the nearby slum or live on the streets. I have spent many nights without food and I understand when they say they do not have money. They settle their bills when they get money. I do not turn away the hungry,' he says.

But many of his customers are also officegoers from the surrounding swanky complexes, who have slowly become acquainted with him. 'Most do not know my story. When some regular customers read about me a few years ago in a newspaper, they asked me about the incident.' For a few moments, they probably differentiated him from all the other invisible people they interacted with every day but knew nothing about.

A good friend in the city is now a street dog, his only family in Mumbai. The dog remains curled up around his feet all day, guarding him loyally if someone approaches the stall where he also sleeps at night. Only in the monsoon, Sadashiv picks up his threadbare bedspread from his cabinet and finds a parked truck to sleep in.

But this life he has built remains illegal in the eyes of the municipality—like tens of thousands of other street vendors, Sadashiv does not have a licence, and faces action by municipal and police authorities at regular intervals. The state government has capped the number of licences to be given to hawkers at 2.5 per cent of the total population and the process of issuing new licences has not begun. Until then, Sadashiv knows he has to face the brunt of his belongings being hauled off by anti-encroachment squads, but says these events wear him down. 'Sometimes, the action taken is so severe that we are detained for several hours, left to beg and plead to be released with our seized belongings. Usually, a hefty fine is applied. There have been times when there is no information about where the team has taken the belongings. A few months ago, I had to go all the way to Mulund to get my stuff back,' he says. On such days, he incurs losses on his perishable items. On days that he is alerted about the municipal van doing the rounds, he suspends his work even if he is midway into cooking a meal for a customer.

As Mumbai changes rapidly around him, with the former mill lands around his stall in Worli having been replaced by swank commercial high-rises, action by the municipality has become more frequent. Those buying or selling these luxury spaces do not want the eyesore of poor street vendors, he says. Two recent incidents left him without work for over a week: the first was a stampede at nearby Elphinstone railway station, later renamed Prabhadevi station, and then a huge fire inside the adjacent commercial complex called Kamala Mills. Both tragedies cost human lives, and the authorities' reaction was to crack down on those doing business on the crowded streets. There have been some threats of criminal action too. Begging with the authorities to be let off has become an indignity he dreads. 'It is more difficult than earning my living. I know I do not have the licence currently, but I hope there can be some consideration on humanitarian grounds by the state,' Sadashiv says. 'I do not intend to do this forever, but I hope I can go on without much trouble till my children graduate and complete their education,' he says. 'I cannot think of taking any other job. I have not studied, I have been on my own in the city for many years. I am scared I will never be comfortable with a job in an office,' he says.

His children are his constant worry and biggest hope. Despite his very meagre income, Sadashiv ensures that both Omkar in Class IX and Jyoti in Class VII attend an English-medium school. Omkar is at a residential school nearly 40 km away from their village, visiting his mother only once a month. In phone conversations with them, Sadashiv listens keenly at the new things they are learning in school and yields to any requests that he can afford. 'Omkar recently wanted a hockey stick. He told me he enjoyed the game and he was good at it, playing at inter-school competitions. I asked him to come to Mumbai with a relative. Omkar and I went to a sports shop near Metro Cinema and I bought him the hockey stick,' Sadashiv smiles. 'I wanted him to have it, but I also wanted him to know where the money came from. So I brought him to my stall and he saw what I do throughout the day.'

His wife and daughter have also visited, to get acquainted with his work. 'When my daughter came to Mumbai for her first visit, she was confident unlike my first time. She wanted to see all the places she had heard about. I took a few days off work and took her around, showing her the city like a tourist, including the Gateway of India, Girgaum Chowpatty,' he says.

Rekha is a superb cook, he declares, revealing a long-held aspiration he has, to work with her in Mumbai, running a meal-on-wheels stall. Her fare would be nonvegetarian, he says of her specialty. Omkar has spoken of joining the military, while Jyoti has said she'd like to join the police force. 'All my hopes remain on them. I cannot stop thinking sometimes about the terror attack, of what I saw that night, of how I almost died. I got a second life, I only hope that my children have better lives.'

* * *

In the last ten years as Rajkumari learnt how to be a single parent in a teeming Mumbai slum, her foremost concern was how to make their children's lives easier than theirs had been, something she and Shivshankar had discussed often. The family learnt to survive as a team, but it has been an uphill climb. She recalls how often Shivshankar's daily earnings sufficed only to buy flour and salt. 'Most nights, I would serve that to the children so they didn't sleep hungry. My husband and I would take a few bites if there were any, or sleep without eating.'

Today, Rajkumari opens the small refrigerator in their one-room home to point at the dark pink, ripe pomegranates she has bought for Sheetal, nineteen, her youngest. 'My children had never seen fruit earlier. It was a luxury.' Sheetal was hospitalized recently and diagnosed with various deficiencies. 'I want to ensure that the children eat healthy. It is so difficult to convince them to eat,' she complains, while Sheetal laughs, only half convincing her mother that she will begin to eat fruit.

'How will you have the energy to study and work if you don't eat?' the mother persists, to more laughter.

Though Shivshankar had been keen to provide the children an education, the poverty had led the children to drop out when he was still alive. With charitable organizations pitching in to cover educational expenses after 2008, Rajkumari enrolled them back.

Eldest son Deepak, now twenty-three, works at a mall in nearby Chembur, earning a little over Rs 10,000 per month. Deepak maintains a tight budget—every month, Rs 3000 from his salary is deducted as an installment for a motorbike he bought a few years ago. The remaining he hands over to his mother. Deepak wishes occasionally that he could spend his earnings like some other youngsters do, maybe catch a film in a cinema hall with friends. At his current job, Deepak is allowed to watch one film a month at the multiplex inside the mall he works at. But money is tight and on holidays he does odd jobs, including fixing electrical appliances or wiring to make a little extra cash that he saves up for his own expenses.

As the only earning member of the family and the eldest sibling at home now with his eldest sister married and looking after her own baby girl, Deepak is also is the go-to person for his two younger siblings. Sandeep is doing a computer hardware repair course at a government-run Industrial Training Institute while Sheetal is pursuing a BCom degree. Deepak's coming of age was also hastened by a train accident in 2010 that nearly killed him. Working as a medicine delivery boy, Deepak was coming home from work during the evening peak hours, and tried to enter a crowded train. 'I fell off the train and was home for a month due to the injuries. For the first time, I realized that I could not take such risks, my family had to be taken care of,' he says.

Rajkumari still has periods of great anxiety, mainly about the family's life in their current surroundings.

The family lives in Annabhau Sathe Nagar, a slum sprawl named after a Dalit folk poet and social reformer. Rajkumari lives with her three children and mother-in-law in a one-room tenement with a double cot on one side and a small kitchen in the opposite corner. Buckets and drums of stored water are lined up along one wall. A photograph of Shivshankar is on another wall, noting the date of his death.

'Everyone thinks we got a lot of money as compensation. Ten years is a long time. Do people think the money changed our lives? Even now, each time we are called for any function related to the terror attacks, when we return, neighbours think we have been given money and we are packing currency notes in our cupboards. How do we explain that we don't even have enough money to buy a room here? We still live in a rented room,' she says. After the attack, when the then home minister R.R. Patil had visited their home, she had requested to be helped with a house. She's still hopeful of getting a small room of their own so that the children have a secure roof over their heads.

'The area we live in does not have access to basic amenities. The paucity of water, space, money, ends up causing fights among residents. It is so easy to get aggressive and into a fight. As a single parent, I would earlier always be on edge about my children getting involved in a fight. What if it took an ugly turn or if they were caught by the police for no fault of theirs?' Rajkumari says. This, she says, made her turn down an offer of employment after her husband's death. 'In all these years, I have never been involved even in an argument with anyone here. You can ask the neighbours,' she says.

In fact, the goodwill she has earned means that many around her keep an eye on the children for her. For example, a neighbour once reprimanded Deepak for speeding on his bike and doing stunts on it with friends.

She says, 'I know that my husband must be looking from above, feeling happy that his children are studying. Ten years is a long time to be without him. I now think of how such a long time passed; how did the children grow up; how did I bring them up? Maybe it's him up there ensuring that we are fine.'

D.L.N. Reddy, *Untitled*, etching and aquatint, 1998
Collection: DAG

8

From Adversity to Opportunity

Aaron Pereira

For many in India, the evening of 26 November 2008 was spent watching India defeat visitors England in a one day international cricket match in Cuttack, Odisha. In the United States, however, it was a much more spectacular event, the best sky show of the year, and one that enthralled many, including Kia Scherr, then fifty-two, who watched the lunar spectacle from her Florida home and thought what she was seeing on the evening sky was the moon and two stars below it. Except that it wasn't two stars. It was a rare three-way conjunction of Venus, Jupiter and a crescent moon.

That moonlit night in Florida, Kia had just confirmed that her husband Alan and teenage daughter Naomi were at the Oberoi Hotel in South Mumbai when it was attacked by terrorists armed with automatic weapons and grenades. Alan and Naomi were part of a twenty-five-member meditation group called Synchronicity that was visiting Mumbai in 2008 for a spiritual interaction. They were dining at The Tiffin, a restaurant on the ground floor of the five-star property overlooking the Arabian Sea at Nariman Point when terrorists stormed into the restaurant. Diners inside The Tiffin were among the first casualties that night.

'Astronomers from all over the world were waiting for that evening's moon because Jupiter and Venus were positioned right under it. It was a crescent moon. It almost looked like a smile. I remember, we went out to look at the moon and we initially thought there were two bright stars under the moon, and my sister said, "Look, there's Alan and Naomi". And I said, "That's how we will always remember them."'

Kia says she didn't know it then, but that celestial moment changed her life. 'I think it was very significant for me. It was the culmination of an astronomical event but it was also the end of life for me as I knew it at that point. I had to find a way to come back to life and it was Mumbai that brought me back to life.'

After two frantic days of trying to verify the whereabouts of her husband and daughter, it was only on Friday, 28 November 2008, that Kia could confirm her worst fears. Thirty-two people had died in The Tiffin, twenty-two guests and ten staffers. Thirteen-year-old Naomi was found dead under a dining table where she'd been hiding. Alan, fifty-eight, was found nearby, a gunshot to his head.

Even as the news sank in, images of Ajmal Kasab, the lone surviving terrorist, were flashed repeatedly on her television screen in Florida.

'As I was just staring at this young man, I felt that there's enough hate. We need to send love and compassion and we need to forgive, so that we can move on. Everything was cracked open and what I learnt in that moment is the core essence of what it means to be human—that love still exists,' Kia says now.

It was in that moment of adversity that Kia gained the strength to forgive.

Somehow certain that she had a responsibility to spread her message of love and forgiveness, Kia set up the One Life Alliance (OLA) in 2009, a foundation that highlights the sacredness of life and seeks to counter hatred and extremism with messages of peace. Another year later, Kia arrived in Mumbai—her first visit to a city that would go on to become her second home—to launch the Mumbai chapter of the organization. Along with her were several members of Synchronicity, including some who were survivors of the 26/11 attacks. 'We launched One Life Alliance in the regal room of the Trident, then the Oberoi, on the anniversary of the attacks. Twelve of the twenty-five members of Synchronicity who had been in Mumbai that night came back,' she says.

Since then, Kia has been on a mission, beginning in Mumbai but one she hopes will soon become global. Mumbai is where she lost her family and yet, she says, it is where she feels at home. 'Every time I went there, I felt welcomed as a family member. I felt comfort. I was nurtured by the spirit of Mumbai. I know some will say it is a cliché but it is also true. There is a genuine spirit of Mumbai—it's the spirit of love. Love is what survived the horrific attacks which had terror embedded in it. Love is what strengthened the city and love is what helped people overcome their grief. It is that which unites us all.'

The One Life Alliance's work with organizations and schools across the world is backed by the Anne and Joe Slicker Foundation. Joe, then eighty-seven, was also a survivor of the 26/11 attacks, having been in Mumbai on the meditation tour. Close friends of the Scherrs, the Slicker family has been backing One Life Alliance ever since its inception in 2009. Joe himself passed away in 2016.

Joe's son, John, based in Texas, recalls the forty-eight hours he spent locked inside a room at Oberoi Hotel waiting to be rescued. John had decided to skip dinner that evening and headed to his room. His father and a friend joined him as soon as gunshots were heard. All three remained holed up in their rooms, a forty-hour wait, even as their rooms filled with smoke, until they were rescued.

John sees supporting Kia as an opportunity to help change the discourse on terrorism and violence. 'Kia had this idea to start One Life Alliance with Master Charles Cannon. We were ready to support her and the initiative. On the second anniversary of the attacks, at the launch of the OLA, India Chapter, in Mumbai, my father and I went back. There were nine of us who came back to

Mumbai in 2010. John has made several trips to India, having lived in Kolkata in the 1980s. In 2017, he went on a pilgrimage to holy cities across India, including Varanasi and Rishikesh. 'A persisting question is how to reconcile something irreconcilable. A lot of it has to do with acceptance of what's going on, and why. Trusting that there is a purpose to this even though it seems purposeless. And then accepting that,' he says.

* * *

Keep holding on
'Cause you know we'll make it through We'll make it
 through
Just stay strong
'Cause you know I'm here for you I'm here for you

Naomi's favourite song, 'Keep Holding On' by Avril Lavigne, could have been an anthem for Kia and her family. Naomi's cousin and best friend, Samantha Delise, the same age as Naomi and even born in the same month, met her only during family vacations. Naomi lived a secluded life within the Synchronicity meditation community in Virginia, while Samantha lived in Michigan. 'She didn't have any friends her age. We would write each other letters, sharing incidents in our lives and my school and about what new music we were listening to. Naomi's favourite band was Linkin Park—she got lucky and attended one of their concerts with her dad,' Samantha says.

Having been homeschooled through her life, Naomi was preparing to return from Mumbai and join a boarding school in New York, where she wanted to take up poetry and writing.

'We would spend our holidays together at a rented house for a week where we would get a chance to do what other kids our age would. We would step out and swim in the lake. We would dress up as mermaids, catch fireflies together and gather the family in the evening and put on a show. We were really close. My family would play poker and she would cheer on her brothers while I cheered on my brother competitively,' Samantha recalls.

She remembers the phone call that November night. 'It was around Thanksgiving. We were watching a movie when my aunt called and broke the news to us. I remember how excited Naomi was when she coloured her hair turquoise, green and black before she went to Mumbai that year.'

Before leaving on her two-week meditation tour, Naomi, then thirteen, had asked her parents whether she could get a tattoo, something she had wanted for a long time. While her parents refused, saying she could get one when she turned eighteen, they allowed her to get a nose piercing during her trip to India. 'I've got two piercings on my nose now,' Samantha says.

Kia's sons Aaron and Adam, twenty-six and twenty-four years old in 2008, got tattoos though. 'One of a heart with two wings. They were both deeply wounded by the attacks and are to this day. It has had a very deep impact,'

Kia says, adding that Kasab was just about the age of her younger son.

* * *

Having had her nose pierced, Naomi, left wide-eyed by Mumbai's fast-paced life and colourful streets, planned an evening out with Linda Ragsdale, an art illustrator also part of the Synchronicity meditation tour. That November evening, Linda was dining with the Scherrs at The Tiffin restaurant when the attack began.

'The bullet entered above my heart, travelled through my spinal column and exited the top of my thigh . . . It left me with a three-foot wound,' Linda recalls, adding that it was an Oberoi staffer who dragged her out to safety once the gunmen were on the higher floors.

Back in the United States, Linda was not going to let the attacks beat her. 'We had these things we wanted to do: break a pool somersault record, get mehndi on our feet and learn how to draw dragons. I didn't get a chance to teach Naomi how to draw that, so I set up the Peace Dragon as a way to fulfil that promise.'

Linda's 'Peace Dragon' project is an art initiative that helps inculcate values of peace among schoolchildren across the world, encouraging them to express themselves through art and mindfully choose peace.

The initial years saw Linda travel the world and give schoolchildren the lens of a 'Peace Dragon' to view the world through, but her challenges were only beginning. In

2015, back from a trip to Japan and excited about a year of travel ahead, Linda was diagnosed with stage three breast cancer and underwent a double mastectomy.

'In true dragon style, I asked my doctor "how do we do this". A day before my surgery I threw this huge party called "lemons to lemonade" and the invitation was a lemon and you had to write your favourite quote and we hung it all over. I wasn't going to let this get the better of me. I couldn't let fear win,' Linda recalls.

Braving cancer was no easy task but Linda took it as a challenge. 'When I had to shave my head, I got my kids to shape a dragon on my head. I didn't even know one lost their eyebrows and eyelashes to chemotherapy. So I decided to share my bald stories with people. Very few want to speak about it. When you wake up in the morning your face is there, but when you have cancer your face is just not there.'

The battle with cancer won, Linda has now begun working on a book about her experiences—the Mumbai attacks, the work she's been doing with schools and her fight with cancer. But 'the universe had different plans and my husband was detected with esophageal cancer last year,' Linda says.

'It's been over a year now since my husband is with cancer. It's one of those cancers that doesn't have an outcome. It came down to how do we change helpless to helpful? How do we change hopeless to hopeful?' Linda says. Her days are now filled with thinking deeply about how not to get sucked into depression.

These exacting experiences, Linda says, have helped prepare her for her next adventure, on creating a museum to make everyone 'mental health literate'. 'We will start off with the first top ten disorders that people are dealing with. We have a patient's story and then have an artist take that story and translate it into the drawing of a dragon. So you have a story, a visual and then you have a doctor come in and help you understand what it is and what you can do. It's about coming to understand how to deal with those holes that are filled with darkness. You could be sitting next to someone who is dealing with a mental health issue and you have no idea about it, especially children,' Linda explains. Along the same lines, Linda and her team are also working on Spark—an anger management app for children and parents. 'Will you become a hothead or will you do something about it? Can you extinguish it yourself? Essentially, a series of questions that help you keep track of anger. Where did it start? Who was involved? How angry did you get? You can help children recognize a trend in a child and how to resolve it,' she says.

Before the attacks that evening, Linda and the Synchronicity team were at a meditation session, chanting a version of the peace mantra 'Om mani padme hum'. And it stuck. 'The boys who walked into the Trident that night were frightened. They walked through the lobby in fear. Where is the divide that we are creating? How did they get to that space?' she wonders.

In September this year, Linda hopes to release the 'Peace Dragon' book, the fifth in her series of illustration books for children. In this story, the protagonists, Omani, the dragon and young explorer, Sherwyn, are named after Naomi and Alan Scherr.

* * *

Perhaps it was Naomi's age that nudged Kia towards schoolchildren, for one of the first projects she launched in Mumbai was popularizing the thirty-day One Life Alliance pledge in schools and colleges across the city, a three-year project that kicked off in 2012. The pledge was in the form of a series of messages of oneness and the sacredness of life. At the Don Bosco High School in Matunga, central Mumbai, where Kia worked closely with the administration, videos were created for each of the thirty messages in the pledge. These were then passed on to teachers from other schools so they could take the life pledge forward.

Kia recalls running into students in the city who would share how the pledge had helped them personally. 'They would tell me how their lives have changed. How it helped them grow closer to their family members . . . to forgive after years of anger.' One student from Don Bosco ended up as a staff member at the Trident Hotel, where Kia lives when she is in Mumbai. 'He came up to me and said my discussion on forgiveness had really changed his life.' For some, it helped bring families riven by hatred and anger back together in peace. 'I was at this cafe when a young girl came up to me and hugged me and she wept, saying, "I was able to forgive my father . . ." She said it just changed the family dynamics—he was an alcoholic and had been very abusive. The pledge had helped her and her mother deal with it in some way.' Another Mumbaikar told her of how a girl who had been abused by her brother and wanted to commit suicide underwent a forgiveness session after which she decided to forgive him. 'Hearing such things gave me the chills because you never know how a simple message based in love is going to impact people and change their lives,' Kia says.

Her message of peace also found resonance in New Delhi where red alerts or terror alerts were sounded every other month. In 2012, following a presentation by Kia at Ramanujan College, a student decided to implement the thirty-day peace pledge, first with her family and then at the Millennium School in Meerut, a small, communally sensitive town on the outskirts of Delhi. In January 2014, the campaign went a step ahead with a 'peace flash mob' held in the national capital where residents were made aware of India's dismal ranking in the Global Peace Index published by the Institute for Economics and Peace, a think tank that analyses peace to correlate it with economic benefits. In 2013, the Index ranked India 142nd among 161 nations. They were then made to take an oath of peace. 'People were invited to take an oath of peace to respect the dignity of life in self and others. It is a lack of respect that is breaking down the structures of peace throughout our society,' Kia said in a Facebook post she shared.

She also penned a letter to Kasab, who was lodged in a Mumbai jail and executed in 2012. He did not get a chance to read the letter, but she hopes it reached him in spirit.

'Who do you think you killed? Who died? You may have destroyed many individual lives for which you need to be accountable, but the sacred life that resides in each of us can never be destroyed, no matter how big and powerful your weapon is. The light that emerged from the ashes of Mumbai began when I first saw your photograph on the news as the lone surviving terrorist. The words of Jesus Christ came to me in those moments—"Forgive them, they know not what they do." I felt compassion for the human being I saw on the TV that was so shrouded in darkness that he forgot who he was.'

The letter, published widely first on social media and then excerpted by newspapers, was met with stunned surprise, a reaction Kia continues to elicit when she tells people she truly forgave those who killed Alan and Naomi. 'There is a lot of misunderstanding about forgiveness. When people say to me "I could never forgive", I understand where they are coming from because I think in their minds it means letting go . . . of something that was an atrocity or a horrific act. Or somehow that forgiving would be excusing it or condoning it, but that is not at all what forgiveness means,' Kia says.

She explains that when she says the loss of those closest to her completely cracked her open, she is referring to 'a journey about what forgiveness actually is'. She understood that the terror attacks in Mumbai were a well-planned operation, one for the justice system to tackle. 'But what is forgiveness? It's about rising above all that and not holding that anger and hatred in my own heart so that I don't become a hostage. I'm not letting them make me live with hate. No way. The only way I can rise above this and honour the lives of my family is to respond with love and forgiveness so that I can be peaceful.' The message of forgiveness is not based in religion, she says, nor is it a choice to make just once. 'It begins with the willingness to heal one's own heart and then it is a process, I would say. The last ten years have been a process . . . Ten years ago I could not have said to you what I said now.'

* * *

Still jousting with her grief, immersed in her own journey, in 2013, the One Life Alliance launched the 'Pocketbook of Peace'. An upgrade from the thirty-day pledge, it had actionable messages to help raise the peace quotient by following simple messages.

Kia took this pocketbook to Mumbai Police and, with the help of a local NGO, set up a 'peace alert' system where thirty Mumbai Police officials would get a message on their phones each morning that had, apart from a quote, three pointers—reminders, challenges and insights on acceptance, trust and forgiveness, among others. These thirty officials would meet every week at the police headquarters where they would discuss how they were implementing these messages in their daily routines. 'It was mostly in Marathi, a few would speak English so I had to have someone translate it for me, but I really felt it was for them to share with one another how it affected their relationship with the community. The whole point was to build trust with the people.'

With that project now disbanded, Kia is looking for funding to continue working with the police force, convinced that the pilot project had a lasting impact on the participating policemen. 'We had them write down some of the things they derived from the daily alerts and they said it helped them handle stress. They said it never occurred to them that you could create a positive outcome by making a positive choice to behave in a certain way.'

Kia is now using this pocketbook as a model of instruction, not just with schools and educational institutions but also with businesses across the world. 'I want to do more with the pocketbook of peace, to get it out to the public through the hotel industry, for instance. That's where people from across the world come. Why can't we have it in every room? It will reach a global audience.'

Could her message of peace reach villages and schools where the 26/11 terrorists were trained? Kia hopes that One Life Alliance will soon reach schools in Pakistan via NGOs working in the field of education. Some early discussions in 2012 had shown promise in this regard.

'It would be great to work with organizations that are already operational so we don't have to start from scratch. We could even have an Urdu version of the pocketbook that could be taken there through the hotel industry. We could have it at the Marriott Hotel, which was bombed in 2008,' Kia says.

Over the past couple of years, the pocketbook of peace has evolved from being only a response to terrorism and extremism and has travelled across the globe. At a school in Mexico City, a programme based on the pocketbook of peace is currently underway. 'A team there has created a system where a private school would agree to sponsor a public school and so children from more wealthy areas and children from poorer areas would all get the same education. It was called the "life-fullness" programme for kids. It was much more than mindfulness because it was using both heart and mind together to create life-fullness,' Kia says.

The pocketbook has been translated into Spanish and four schools have launched the Lifefullness Kids Programme for children as young as five to teenagers.

Kia's team works with teachers and trains them on implementing the pocketbook of peace, one pledge per week. One day, for example, the theme is to 'slow down'. The students do guided meditation for about five to ten minutes, while other affirmative statements are practiced, such as taking one's time, not rushing through, taking time to notice nature, etc. 'You sort of begin to be more aware. Slow down your speech and what you say, so you smile, breathe, have patience.' Kia says this will, in the long run, help youngsters learn to, say, honour agreements. The children also have to share how they applied their lesson, and the outcomes have often helped prevent bullying and fights or resolve one that erupted, often with the perpetrator apologizing, she says.

The Lifefullness Programme has a fee, but schools that purchase this programme agree to sponsor a public school. The programme will soon be translated into English so it can be introduced in Nashville.

Kia plans to expand the Lifefullness Programme by adapting it for business houses, essentially the same but aimed at increasing productivity through guided meditation and other activities and pledges.

* * *

For a country like India where multiple religions and practices coexist, Kia thinks her proposed Reconciliation Programme could do wonders. Currently at the discussion stage with the office of the Archbishop of Canterbury, the Reconciliation Programme will help people of different beliefs and faiths disagree peacefully. 'They get people to disagree well, not to agree on anything, and come to an understanding with each other as human beings and to connect as human beings and bring that back to their communities so they can resolve their conflicts in a peaceful way.'

The programme would help leaders of various communities come together on a single platform and share views. 'There is a lot going on around religious extremism in India so it's important to work with Hindus, Muslims and Christians because if we can infiltrate that divide some more, then some of the young people who might get inspired to become extremists can perhaps move in the other direction,' she says.

That her own family was killed by terrorists makes her particularly invested in this project, inspired by the Rose Castle Foundation in Cumbria, northwest England. The reconciliation process at Rose Castle Foundation uses scriptural reasoning in working with leaders of various faiths. Kia's idea is to dovetail the pocketbook of peace into their process.

There's also a group called the Indo-Pak Peace Project run by two youngsters based in Karachi who Kia now supports. 'They want to start doing more. They have young people from India and Pakistan and they want to do a lot more cross communication and events. One of them is only nineteen years old. We can look at webinars and more programmes online that are not expensive to do. I'd like to help them develop those kinds of platforms,' says Kia.

Despite her infectious enthusiasm and the success of the projects she has kicked off, there have been times when she was close to giving up, exhausted by red tape and just by the sheer size of the challenge ahead.

'I was never really alone, yet I was alone—it was up to me to initiate things. I had to be the one to follow up on things, and at the end of the day, there I was, all by myself. When you set up things by yourself you think 'oh this is going to be so great' and then it doesn't happen because someone isn't available for three weeks or they're travelling and won't be around. Or you go to a meeting and everyone nods in agreement but nothing materializes,' Kia says.

She recalls tiny incidents that kept her motivated.

'You keep going on. There were times when I was crying and didn't know what was the point of being here, doing what I am doing. Then, you know, a simple little thing would happen. Even though I haven't been to India in two years, I'd get a Facebook message from someone in India talking about how something I did changed their life. That's worth its weight in gold. You just can't measure that sort of thing.'

Kia says she owes a great deal to the staffers at the Trident, where she lost her family and where she lives when she's in Mumbai. 'They are so proud of the work I do in their city. It made them feel like they were part of something. And I owe it to them. I owe it to every person who died in that attack. It's not just my husband and my daughter but it's every single one of them, including the police. The whole city was affected; it has never been forgotten.'

While she hasn't been in Mumbai for the last two years, Kia hopes to raise enough funding to be in the city for the tenth anniversary of the attacks as well as push the peace campaign globally. This year Kia will speak at the Parliament of the World's Religions in Toronto—'A Response of Love to an Act of Terror—How to Love like an Extremist'.

The tenth edition of the pocketbook of peace will also be released this year. In addition, Kia will release a book that she has been working on for the past year titled 'Under the Mumbai Moon—Death, Love and Renewal'. 'It was death that brought me to Mumbai, it was love that kept me going back to Mumbai for about six years and then in the process my life was renewed,' she says, adding that the idea of the book is not just to share the experiences that she has had in Mumbai but also to tell the story of how her life has been transformed in the process. 'It is a book where I want to write about how I came back and renewed my life.'

Suhas Roy, *Untitled*, viscosity, 1968
Collection: DAG

9

The Youngest Witness

Srinath Rao

The television is rarely switched off inside the Rotawan household and once Natwarlal Rotawan walks in, only the news channels play. His kids know that they won't be watching movies any time soon. Scanning channels for news of terror strikes or the latest atrocity at the border attributed to Pakistan is Natwarlal's full-time job. And this is what has ensured that he and his daughter Devika are still talked about close to a decade after she was shot in the leg by Ajmal Kasab at Chhatrapati Shivaji terminus.

In June 2009, a ten-year-old Devika had become a media sensation as the youngest person to depose in a special Terrorist and Disruptive Activities (Prevention) Act court in Mumbai, where Kasab faced trial, identifying the Pakistan national as the man who fired indiscriminately at commuters in the station concourse. Since then, the father-daughter duo has become a regular fixture in the news. The rent-a-quote nature of television news and the father-daughter's aggressive views on terrorism, terrorists and Pakistan have made them the go-to talking heads during every new attack.

'*Media apni baat uchalti rehti hai*,' says Natwarlal animatedly. Their views on attacking Pakistan, actively pursuing the masterminds of the November 2008 terror attacks and their unsaid policy of never refusing interviews means they are always sought-after for sound bites.

Since that June afternoon nine years ago, when Devika emerged from the court in the Arthur Road Jail complex— supporting her right leg with crutches—to a frenzy of flashing cameras, a life lived in the limelight has been extraordinarily difficult. In that decade, she has gone from being a dazed young witness with a crew cut to another teenager who can't be dislodged easily from her phone. The skinny girl now has a head full of straight hair that she complains never grew properly after months spent recuperating on bedbug-infected hospitals beds as a child. The family—fifty-four-year-old Natwarlal, his twenty-three-year-old son Akash, and Devika, now nineteen—went from living in Colaba in November 2008 to having had to shift six rented tenements in Bandra East, in suburban Mumbai, since. In that time, Natwarlal's once flourishing dry fruits import business has folded after his partners cheated him. His children, both having have survived life-threatening events, on account of the attack and also on account of illness, remain poorly educated and ill equipped to grapple with adulthood.

But adversity has served to strengthen the family's sense of pride in all that it has endured and believes it continues to contribute to the discourse surrounding terrorism. While Natwarlal's frail chest does not swell, a quickening of his speech indicates his sense of achievement at allegedly having peppered Kasab with abuses at the beginning of his deposition, at allegedly reducing the terrorist and his lawyer Abbas Kazmi 'to tears' during the course of the trial and 'challenging' Pakistan in May after being invited to a felicitation programme in the border town of Sri Ganganagar in Rajasthan.

* * *

Admittedly disinterested in academics as a child, Devika's desire post-26/11 to become an Indian Police Service officer has not yet been backed up by strong grades. Multiple factors, including a lack of interest, the death of her mother Sarika during childbirth in 2006 and an inability to adjust to a school in her native village of Sumerpur, Rajasthan, meant that Devika had more or less abandoned her education until November 2008, when she would under normal circumstances have been studying in Class V.

It would be at least another year before Devika managed to get admitted to a school. Although fast-tracked to Class VII as deemed appropriate for her age, she would lag woefully behind her classmates. 'I didn't understand textbooks or how to write exams because I hadn't been formally schooled. Also, I had to put up with TV news crews coming home and filming me studying,' says Devika.

She is grateful for the intervention of a local political outfit, without whom she says the management of a school in Bandra would not have agreed to admit her. Prior to that, she had been turned down by another English-medium school in the same locality, allegedly owing to her terror tag. By then, the youngster says, she was being dubbed snidely as '*Kasab ki beti*' for identifying him in court. In a television interview she gave in 2010 as an articulate eleven-year-old, she looks resolutely into the camera while claiming that the school was afraid to admit her due to the fear of being attacked by terrorists. The school management had defended its refusal to grant admission claiming that Devika's education up to that point had not prepared her for Class V.

Personal circumstances, however, would continue to intervene and cause gaps in her education. Her brother Akash contracted an infection that put him on bed rest for two years and eventually developed a permanent disability.

'When Devika was admitted to JJ Hospital, I used to clean and dress her wounds. Pretty soon, relatives of the other patients in the ward began to complain to the nurses and the doctors that I was only taking care of Devika. I was then forced to clean the wounds of the other patients in the ward as well,' says Akash.

The family says that the boy, then barely in his teens, used his bare hands to attend to open cuts and soon caught an infection that began innocuously with a bout of tonsils. 'He was very careless and did not take care of his own safety. He did not use gloves or clean his hands properly after attending to a patient,' Devika says of the beginning of her brother's ordeal.

Things became grim when Akash had to be operated upon for a bone poking out of his rib cage—the infection had affected his spine, making it curve painfully just below the neck. Their father estimates that he spent close to Rs 17 lakh to treat Akash—and this was after the collapse of his dry fruits business bankrupted him. The disability also put paid to any serious efforts by Akash to finish his education. Last year, he appeared for his Class X exams privately, but studying proved extremely difficult. 'I wasn't able to attend classes because that involved sitting in one place for seven or eight hours a day. I either need to stand for some time or lie down for some time,' he says. He didn't pass.

The next time Devika found a measure of stability she was struck with a severe bout of tuberculosis in 2016. With the family now severely cash-strapped and compensation money received from the state government and the Indian Railways amounting to about Rs 3.2 lakh long exhausted, she spent a year and half petitioning Maharashtra Chief Minister Devendra Fadnavis for financial assistance. 'If I had died then no one would remember me,' says Devika, with a hint of bitterness. The CM's dole of Rs 10 lakh helped her pay for the treatment and in rejoining school.

In the first week of June this year, at the age of nineteen, Devika finally completed the first phase of her education, passing the Class X board exams with a 50 per cent score. 'I didn't do well in Hindi and Marathi so I was expecting to score this much,' she says. She has already started attending coaching classes for a fresh attempt at the language exams next month while also starting work on familiarizing herself with subjects in the Arts stream that she plans to opt for in junior college. For now, though, she is like any other student in the city on the cusp of starting college, in equal parts anxious and excited, applying to colleges and shopping for books, stationery supplies and a college-ready wardrobe.

* * *

Inside the Rotawan family's rented ground-plus-one house in Subhash Nagar, Bandra East, located behind the school where Devika has graduated from, a row of awards and framed certificates placed in rows above the television immediately draws the eye.

Circular and rectangular frames, awards, citations, medals—even a solid metal Nandi bull—take up a lot of space on the wall above the bed, which occupies a large portion of their ground floor living quarters. 'We have a big cardboard carton full of more awards, shawls and shirt pieces upstairs,' says Akash, seated on the narrow stairs to the upper floor where Devika is cooking rotis for lunch.

A couple of frames are propped up on boxes that Akash has covered with bright chart paper, lending a dash of colour to the yellow wall. 'I've always had a liking for crafts. Those are meter boxes and the chart paper not only hides them but also saves us the trouble of putting another nail into the wall, which the landlord won't appreciate,' he laughs. A recurring work of the young man is a poster with his sister's name and the numerals 26/11 painted in large, bold letters. Stuck on a side are pictures of Devika with Fadnavis, and actors Amitabh Bachchan and Saif Ali Khan. 'I have made a new poster each time we have moved to a different house,' says Akash.

By their own admission, the family has attended between 550 and 600 functions held in Devika's honour since 2009. Starting with Worli in June 2009, when a social activist hosted an evening to celebrate 'the youngest witness', it has been at least two functions a month since then. Devika prefers to call them shows.

'At these shows my father and I are the only 26/11 survivors invited to speak,' she explains. The shows have taken the family all over their native Rajasthan, Madhya Pradesh and increasingly to Raipur, Chhattisgarh. Each time Devika is invited as a guest of honour at a programme in a different corner of the country to salute her bravery, she recounts her experiences, with a standard opening line: 'I was nine years and eleven months old at the time. On that day, we were to go to Pune to stay with my oldest brother (Bharat). We planned to roam around Pune and have a lot of fun. We were also going to meet my aunt, stay with her and return to Mumbai after a few days. We reached CST at night and sat waiting on the platform when Akash said that he needed to go to the toilet. My father told him to go and that he would buy tickets in the meantime. But as soon as Akash left, I saw a bomb explode and heard the sound of gunfire. One bullet hit me in the right leg and I fell down. Before passing out I saw a gunman firing indiscriminately . . .'

She goes on to describe waking up to sights of people in terrible pain at St George Hospital, enduring an agonizing wait to be operated upon before being shifted to JJ Hospital, where doctors tended to her broken leg. She ends her account with the Mumbai Police Crime Branch contacting her father early in 2009 regarding his willingness to become a prosecution witness in Kasab's trial.

It is then her father's turn to speak. 'I usually fill in the gaps that she has left in the story or some facts she omitted by mistake or not narrated in chronological order,' says Natwarlal. The well-oiled speech machine has rolled on in Indore, Ujjain, Bhopal, Ratlam, Jaipur, Bikaner, Pali, Sri Ganganagar, Raipur, Pune and Solapur. 'Once when we were returning to Mumbai from Rajasthan, a group met us at Jodhpur station where our train had stopped, and felicitated us,' beams Natwarlal. 'In fact,' adds Akash, 'we just haven't been invited anywhere in south India yet.'

In attendance at these shows, where Natwarlal claims crowds chant 'Jhansi ki Rani Devika', are Members of Parliament, local Members of Legislative Assembly, IAS and IPS officials, important and local dignitaries, wealthy residents and a mix of athletes and Bollywood celebrities. 'The only people we are yet to meet are the Prime Minister and President,' says Devika.

The collection of awards continues to grow even as the print fades from the first one she picked up in Mumbai in 2009. Most depict smiling portraits of Devika alongside messages of inspiration, admiration or congratulation, and pictures of the burning Taj Mahal Hotel. Some also bear pictures of Swami Vivekananda and Guru Nanak, depending on the organization that has chosen to honour her.

The most prized of these possessions is stacked in a cardboard box kept on the floor below the TV—a wooden plaque inlaid with gold and silver bearing the legend 'Rajasthan Ratan Award'. 'This is nothing. We have left the silver swords and heavier awards at our home in the village,' says Akash, who is standing on the bed and wiping dust off the frames hanging closer to the ceiling while his father is polishing the Rajasthan Ratan Award.

The 'samman' or respect as Natwarlal refers to the material accolades, doesn't even include the tonnes of flowers and bouquets that organizers, attendees and admirers at shows saddle Devika with. 'They make garlands larger than those currency note garlands that party workers give Narendra Modi and Mayawati at public rallies,' boasts Natwarlal. The family likes to joke that on their return to Mumbai from each show, they have to book an entire compartment just to store the flowers Devika receives.

The shining awards serve as ideal backgrounds for television interviews that take place inside her home. But Natwarlal would like a permanent and bigger home where he can display them all with the glory they deserve. 'Government officials don't come to see us at our at home because they feel humiliated seeing all the awards that Devika has got over the years,' he fumes.

Apathy on the part of the Maharashtra government has been a constant refrain of the family ever since the news made them household names. And that feeling has only been exacerbated with the unending stream of accolades pouring in from civil society and private organizations. It is high time, feels Natwarlal, that the country and the world does something for his daughter.

As an example, the family talks about a recent show in Indore where senior police and Army officers 'saluted' Devika. Several shows end with the organizations handing large cheques like those handed to the man of the match at cricket matches, while smaller voluntary donations are made by other attendees.

'All we have been asking for from the state government is a house and for Devika's educational expenses to be taken care of. But the government of Maharashtra has done nothing,' complains Natwarlal.

Akash forwards a slightly different theory. 'The Maharashtra government tells us that the Government of Rajasthan should fulfill our needs because we are natives of that state. On the other hand, Rajasthan says that Maharashtra should take responsibility because that is the state we live in and where Devika was shot. *In dono ke beech mein* Devika *pis rahi hai* (Devika's chances are in a churn between these two government),' he says.

The family manages to pay the rent and meet the daily expenses through the doles received from their appearances and by Natwarlal working for a couple of hours every morning and evening at a general store run by a cousin in Subhash Nagar.

Seated on the bed and sweeping his hands in a wide arc above his head to point out Devika's awards, Natwarlal insists that his demand to the government is not about money.

'*Yeh sab milkar hum ko koi fayda nahi hua. In se hamare pet ko shanti nahi hua hai.* Awards *se pet thodi na bharta hai.* (The awards have not benefited us. You can't survive on awards.) Even if the government gives us Rs 10 crore it won't be enough,' he says. For a key witness in a landmark terror trial to live in squalid rented accommodations sullies India's global image, he says in agitation.

In stark contrast, alleges Natwarlal, the state government gave homes and financial assistance to families of senior police officials killed in the attacks.

'This is the girl who got Kasab the death penalty. What has the government done for her?' he asks.

The family's feeling of utter neglect has been hardened by what it claims are a series of tall and unfulfilled promises by top politicians in the previous and present dispensation. They recount incidents of power brokers ferrying them to bungalows of top leaders and ministers only to endure a lengthy wait and having to leave each time with hasty explanations that 'sahab cannot meet you today' ringing in their ears all the way back to their slum in Bandra East.

'*Ek se ek jano ne humko sirf uloo banaya* hai. *Sab ne sirf badi badi baatein ki hai. Aap bhi sirf waada karke chale mat jaana* (many people have taken us for a ride after making tall promises. I hope you will keep your promise),' says Devika.

Even at the shows that the family is invited to, they claim the organizers promise to send them large sums of money. *Woh log baat karte karodo ki hai par haath mein sirf kuch lakh hi aate hain* (they make tall claims of crores of rupees, but we ultimately receive a few lakhs),' rues Natwarlal.

The most recent promise was made by their hosts in Sri Ganganagar, who pledged to spend Rs 5 crore for a lavish ceremony whenever Devika chooses to marry. 'I only believe these claims when I see a cheque,' he adds.

* * *

Natwarlal's keen eyes hardly leave the television screen when a news item of his interest airs. 'I grasp the story in a few minutes and say what the reporters do not or cannot say on TV,' he exclaims proudly.

He swears to having knowledge beforehand of Kasab's execution late in 2012, much before authorities confirmed it to the press. 'By the time reporters called me that morning, I told them I already knew that Kasab was going to be hanged. Why? Because he killed so many people and he deserved nothing less than the death penalty,' he explains.

It is this, the theory that a convicted terrorist deserves to be hanged until dead that Natwarlal claims as his accuracy in predicting the demise of condemned men. 'People told me that I was mad when I said that Afzal Guru would be hanged. But I stuck to my belief that he would and what

I said came true within two days of me saying it publicly,' he says.

Among his accurate predictions, Natwarlal also counts the hanging of Yakub Memon, much like the half-hearted belief in the powers of prediction of the Paul, an octopus living in the fish tank in Germany, who famously prophesied the victory of Spain in the 2010 FIFA World Cup. The names remaining now on Natwarlal's list are of Lashkar-e-Taiba founder Hafiz Saeed, alleged 26/11 plotter Zaki-ur Rehman Lakhvi and fugitive don Dawood Ibrahim.

His brush with terror, he claims, began in 1995, when he was abducted by henchmen working for gangster Dawood Ibrahim for refusing to pay them a hafta of Rs 10 lakh. 'That was hardly a big amount of money for me at the time. But, like my father and grandfather, I do not believe in giving money to those who do not deserve it. If I have some extra money, I would rather give it to the poor,' he says.

While there is no police complaint of what followed, Natwarlal claims to have been confined in an apartment in Colaba and thrashed mercilessly for three days. When he continued to resist, the men let him go, he claims. Natwarlal refused to register a complaint with the police, he claims, as that would mean the end of a prosperous first-generation dry fruits business he had established in Colaba just ten years previously. His wife Sarika would eventually nurse him back to health. '*Dawood mera dushman hai* (Dawood is my enemy),' he says. Sarika died in 2006 after a brief illness.

His business continued to grow until November 2008. 'I kept on accepting orders on phone while in the hospital and asked fellow traders to help deliver my consignments. When I was finally able to go to the market to pick up my cash, the traders refused to give me my money. They said that they did not want to do business with me any more because of the terror attacks,' he says.

Stung by the betrayal, Natwarlal wrote to the police and state government for assistance, only to be left on his own. 'I had to pay the supplier Rs 5 crore from my own pocket by selling my house. That brought us on the road,' he says. Increasingly, his relatives in Mumbai and Rajasthan also begun to shun him, for fear that they might be attacked by terrorists as a result of the association.

A bankrupt father to two young and ailing children, he saw a way out by becoming a prosecution witness. 'I thought that maybe appearing in court for the police would help solve my problems,' he admits. On the one hand, while his personal tragedies continued to mount, the resultant fame only pushed his family away further. 'My uncle stopped me from entering my village unless I gave him a lot of money. He thought I had become rich by giving interviews and going to award shows. But if I had made money, I would not be standing in a queue every time I wanted to go to the toilet,' he says.

For Devika, the obsession has more to do with seeing herself as a part of the solution. '*IPS officer banke sab ki dhajiyan uda degi* (she'll become an Indian Police Service officer and give them a befitting reply),' is Natwarlal's modest expectation.

Talking about terror at every possible public forum and asserting a need for it to be crushed for good has taken precedence over every other activity. 'Each time I have an exam, I am invited to a show. But I can't say no because 26/11 and the country is more important to me than studying. If I stop talking about terror, that means I have forgiven my attacker. If I forget about it and live happily, it is wrong and I cannot do that. My life has changed completely after 26/11. Before this, I was a normal little girl playing all the time, wrapped up in my own world who knew nothing of anything else. After 26/11 I became a different Devika, who thought about the country and wanted to fight against terrorists. I prefer living like this. I don't ever want to forget about 26/11 until terrorism has ended,' she says.

She is acutely aware though that it is only an intense and continuing spotlight that has helped her remain relevant. 'Without all these shows, my name would not be everywhere the way it is today and I would have led a normal life. I would just be another person injured in the attack. I don't think these shows will ever end and it is very important for them to happen and for me to keep giving interviews, so that I can put across my message of fighting terrorism,' she says.

In the same breath, she adds that Kasab's execution did not give her lasting joy. '*Woh toh ek chhota sa machchar tha* (he was like a mosquito). The masterminds of the attacks are still wanted and haven't yet been caught and punished. *Unko phansi lagegi toh lagega ki insaaf hoga.* Until then, more terrorists will come into India and do a repeat of 26/11. Something like that should never happen again in India or anywhere else in the world. That is the main reason why I want to become an IPS officer. I want to do something for the country; be useful for the country,' she says. The family, chips in her father, has made it their mission to see these men dead.

* * *

During particularly painful moments in recounting his struggles thus far Natwarlal's frustration at the inaction of the political class to recognize his daughter's contribution boils over in bizarre fashion. Without breaking stride, he proclaims that only a party that assists Devika can expect victory in elections. 'The Congress party in Rajasthan and Maharashtra did not do anything for her and they lost state elections. Now the BJP is in power in both states and at the Centre but they haven't done anything for her either. The BJP will also lose power if they make false promises to us,' he insists.

Half of Devika's dozen tweets on her Twitter account are pleas addressed to Prime Minister Narendra Modi for a meeting. 'Modiji keeps says "*beti bachao, beti padhao*". *Main bhi toh beti hoon.* He watches the news a lot so he surely knows about me. My dream is to meet him,' she says.

Natwarlal's criticism is a lot more pointed. 'No one bothers about a PM after the end of his five-year term. No one interviews him. A Prime Minister should do something for which he will be remembered after his term, like Devika has done,' he says.

Natwarlal is at pains to point that out Devika's case is a world apart from others who have suffered in the aftermath of November 2008. 'Many others have not come forward to speak up because they are either afraid of the consequences or want something in return. But this is a girl who has stuck to her stand for nine years,' he says.

'Even today,' he goes on, 'television news channels from America, China and Indonesia come to interview us because we have never stepped away from this case. *Hum kabhi hate nahi* (we never backed off).'

In Natwarlal's estimation, people the world over recall 26/11 quicker than they do 9/11 or the terror attacks perpetrated by the Islamic State, solely because of his daughter's testimony. In return, he wants her daughter to be felicitated at the hands of the President and Prime Minister. 'I'm not saying she should get the Bharat Ratna. That is not our target. But do something that helps her in her life ahead,' he says.

Somnath Hore, *Untitled*, etching and engraving, 1983
Collection: DAG

10

When Survivors Connect

Kavitha Iyer

Like his personal hero Captain Jack Sparrow, Rohan Kamble, nineteen, is a bit of a nomad in the making. In the last days of December 2017, he decided to usher in the new year with a trip to Mantralayam, a little temple village deep inside Andhra Pradesh's Kurnool district. It would be a week's holiday, he told his mother, before going on to stay twenty-five days, with a friend, in a little room offered by the latter's relative. He watched YouTube videos to assemble a stove with bricks and firewood, learnt to cook his own food, and spent the days rambling about the countryside, being shocked at the bountiful wildlife and the general impoverishment around. He also ended up watching Jumanji in a local cinema hall, dubbed in Telugu. Eventually, he returned home to Mumbai, but with a new friend and fellow traveller, a young boy from Kurnool who had never been to the financial capital. The guest was then dutifully taken around the city-sights—Haji Ali, Bandra-Worli Sea Link, Mukesh Ambani's residence Antilia and the 'vroom-vroom' of a passing Lamborghini Aventador on Marine Drive.

Travelling, Rohan says, is not just a passion, but also a recognition that he has somehow managed to fashion for himself some rather normal growing up years despite the setback of losing his father as a boy. On the night of 26 November 2008, his father Rajan Kamble, a maintenance department staffer at the Taj Mahal Palace and Tower Hotel, was herding a row of guests to safety when a bullet hit his abdomen. Soon after, he was pulled into a nearby room where guests were hiding, and a doctor among the frightened guests tried her best to stanch the flow of blood from his ripped intestines. Having tried serviettes and napkins, she spent the remaining hours of the siege until their evacuation at 9 a.m. on 27 November holding her hand against the wound to keep pressure on it. Through those nerve-racking ten hours, seated nearby just a few feet away from Rajan was journalist and writer Bhisham Mansukhani, who was at the Taj that night with his mother to attend a friend's wedding. A week later, Rajan died in a city hospital.

Bhisham would meet Rohan, his mother Shruti and brother Atharva eight years afterwards, on 26 November 2016, at *The Indian Express* Stories of Strength event at Kala Ghoda in South Mumbai. There was an audiovisual exhibition, and the Kambles had briefly viewed a clip in which Bhisham spoke eloquently about the futility of the death penalty, and of the tense siege that night. After that first meeting, Bhisham would invite the Kambles on a trip to Panchgani, a week that set in motion many new ideas for Rohan—to travel, to reclaim his childhood, and to dare to dream.

Rohan sees himself as the man of the house, and Shruti agrees that in many ways her boys looked after her in the initial years after Rajan's death. Whenever Shruti had to leave them alone for a few hours in their suburban Mumbai home as she went to complete various legal and financial chores, it was Rohan who looked after himself and Atharva, only two years old at the time of the attack. Atharva was sickly for nearly two years afterwards, and again Rohan stepped up to share the caregiving responsibilities. Shruti was herself high-strung for years, often unable to sleep and always fretful about whether her parenting was satisfactory. 'Panchgani really changed a lot of things for me. It was also when the travel bug bit me,' says Rohan. 'It was sheer luck that we met Bhisham Sir, it was the starting point of many good things.'

* * *

As Bhisham Mansukhani and his mother were escorted out of the Taj on the morning of 27 November 2008, rescued from their hiding place by commandos, they emerged from their ordeal to a flurry of questions from journalists, a sleepy police constable noting down their most basic details—there was no debriefing and definitely no personnel trained to deal with traumatized terror survivors—and somebody offering the relieved group Marie biscuits to eat. He had to figure out how to get home. And his mother was barefoot, having lost her sandals in the melee outside the Chambers in the brief minutes when they were taking gunfire. Amid the confusion, Bhisham remembered to check on Rajan. He was told the Taj staffer was being rushed to hospital. A few days later, he found out that the brave gentleman hadn't made it, and thought immediately that he, and perhaps other survivors who had been huddled together in the Lavender Room, should get in touch with Rajan's family. But the Taj management was helping the grieving family with the formalities at that time, and with Shruti having to deal with family members, her children, the last rites and the strain of accepting condolences from hundreds of strangers, the timing seemed incorrect.

Almost a year later, when he was back at the Taj for its reopening, Bhisham checked with representatives of the hotel, and was glad on being told that the Kambles were being cared for, and that Shruti Kamble would never need to worry about the two boys' school or college fees.

'After a while, a sense of shame crept in that I had not reached out, and the thought that what could I possibly do now,' says Bhisham, 'and so I never did establish contact with them despite the thought crossing my mind several times.'

A few years later, in 2012, he reconnected with Initiatives of Change, a network of members from across the world who use introspection and discussion through seminars and conferences to reaffirm their commitment to humanity and building trust across diverse cultures. In India, they are based at a sprawling campus called the Asia Plateau in Panchgani, about 250 km from Mumbai. He had attended their conferences earlier at the Asia Plateau. 'In 2012, I rejoined as volunteer and facilitator. The course director, who I was close to, suggested that I could invite the Kambles for the youth conference.' The idea of sharing their story, their invisible connection appealed to Bhisham, but things did not materialize just then. 'I didn't act on it, and honestly didn't know how,' he says.

Then in 2016, Bhisham and the Kambles were both featured, separately, in *The Indian Express*'s Stories of Strength, an effort to honour terror survivors' resilience and humanity in the face of tremendous loss. On 26 November 2016, at the venue of an audiovisual exhibition and panel discussion hosted by the newspaper, Bhisham was introduced to the Kambles.

Eight years had passed. On every anniversary of the attacks, Shruti had woken at 3 a.m. to prepare for the journey from their home in Gorai, a far suburb of Mumbai, to the Taj, 50 km away. Every year, she had completed her small pre-dawn ritual of a pooja and an offering of a simple meal and two things Rajan loved— masala chai and kaju katli—placed on a tray on her terrace sill for the birds to carry away. And every year, she had felt besieged by questions. Though she had over time heard several accounts, including some from her late husband's colleagues, of how he had died, she had somehow never had the opportunity to talk to any of the over three dozen people in that room with Rajan that night. When she was told Bhisham was attending the event too and that she could meet him, she could barely contain her emotions.

Bhisham spoke gently, describing in exacting detail the events of that night. Rajan had been bravely escorting the guests out of the Chambers from where small batches of guests were being very quietly led to safety. But the terrorists had surprised them at the moment that they were walking in a single file in the corridor outside the Chambers. Rajan was shot even as he pushed somebody out of harm's way, an AK-47 bullet tearing through his back and lower abdomen, ripping out his intestines. Despite the darkness and the ensuing scramble, somebody managed to drag Rajan to safety into one of the rooms along the corridor—the Lavender Room. Bhisham told Shruti that Rajan had been incredibly brave to not cry out in pain—in the pitch black of the room that night, their safety depended on staying hidden. He told her his mother had prayed, seated nearby. Bhisham himself was just across the couch where guests had laid Rajan. Rohan and younger brother Atharva, then seventeen and ten, stood listening intently, but calm. They were all standing actually, the grave, whispered conversation having begun as soon as introductions were over, before they could even sit.

'*Kuch bole kya?* Did he say anything?' she asked repeatedly, unmindful now of tears streaming down her cheeks.

'He spoke only to give us the names of Taj staffers who had escaped, who we should contact so they could send help to our location. Though he was in great pain, he didn't scream even once. At one point he was chanting god's name,' Bhisham told Shruti. Her husband's bravery had saved them that night, he said.

Wiping tears, she told him she'd waited eight years to hear this account. 'Many people told me he had been brave, but this is the first time I am meeting someone who was with him then and saw everything that happened. I knew Rajan was completely selfless and courageous, and now I have heard first-hand what he did.'

Meeting Bhisham was a moment of catharsis and clarity. For she had visited Rajan in a South Mumbai hospital every day between 27 November and 3 December when he died, but he couldn't speak. The last conversations she had had with her husband were by means of facial expressions and nods and grunts that he managed.

On his part, Bhisham remembers being overwhelmed by a sense of sadness at that meeting. 'I honestly cannot begin to imagine the extent of their loss and grief. One could not control what happened and the fact that she had lost her husband, but it was sadder that they were still grieving after eight years. I felt deeply sad that they were still suffering. And I felt, once again, a sense of shame that I had not reached out to them earlier. I apologized, though Shruti did not seem to resent the delay.'

But even as he was speaking to them, he had the idea of inviting them to the youth conference, and a week later he got in touch with them and asked all three if they would visit Panchgani in mid-2017. They agreed. It was going to be the first real holiday out of Mumbai for the mother and her two sons since losing Rajan.

* * *

The Asia Plateau, the India home of the Initiatives of Change, calls itself a centre for 'introspection and dialogue'. Under the aegis of the Initiatives of Change, various smaller groups hold conferences and training programmes, including Let's Make a Difference, which gathers teenagers from across India every year for regional and national youth conferences where scores of youngsters gather to talk about themselves, their inter-personal relationships, their connection with family, their inner demons, career plans, goals and more. The conference uses a blend of reflection, time designated for the participants to spend alone, and discussion to bring about a self-awareness that's not always easy to achieve.

At Asia Plateau, Shruti and Atharva spent time mostly relaxing while Rohan participated in the conference. Atharva discovered some hill trails, species of butterflies and birds he'd never seen in Mumbai and dazzling sunsets viewed from the famous Panchgani tableland. From the weather to the living quarters, Atharva couldn't have asked for a better holiday, he says. 'It was unbelievable.'

Rohan was completely immersed in the conference, participating enthusiastically and making new friends every day of the week-long trip. At one session when participants were encouraged to share stories about their families, he hugged Bhisham and cried profusely. But the biggest take-home for him was the dozens of new connections he made.

Turning eighteen just around then, Rohan found himself truly coming of age. 'There was a clear change in my mindset that came from making new friends from different backgrounds,' he says. While math and algebra were his 'dushman' or enemies through school, he also sailed through other subjects with last-minute cramming. A natural at winning people over, his journal submissions were routinely done by doting friends, all girls. 'No boy will ever do anything like that, no matter how friendly,' he laughs. Completing his education and getting a job, he had always assumed through his school years, were things that would happen in good time, in a natural enough progression of things without him having to expend any special energies.

That outlook changed dramatically, and abruptly, when he returned from Panchgani in the summer of 2017 with a new friends' circle that included youngsters who were focused and determined.

His father and he had briefly considered a career for him in the armed forces, and even a possible stint at a Sainik school, the latter idea being dropped soon after the terror attack as it was immediately clear that Shruti would keep the two boys as close to her as she possibly could, at all times. Later, even while speaking to *The Indian Express* in 2016, Rohan was toying with the idea of a hotel management degree and a job with the Taj group, as a tribute to his late father.

By late 2017, however, he was clear that he would pursue a bachelor of commerce degree while preparing alongside for the company secretaries course. He now repeats exactly what he said then, that he will complete his CS course and work for a couple of years to gather the experience, and then start his own firm. 'What I really want to do is to be able to work for myself. And I don't want to just go with the flow, I want to really give my dreams a shot.'

Bhisham is thrilled that the youth conference left such a lasting impression on Rohan. 'It all comes down to the individual. Hundreds of youth attend that conference and many don't come back. Or others experience a superficial change, an exhilaration after the event. A few return and become an integral part of the organization. It's a personal journey, involving ideas and conversations, but also inner conversations,' Bhisham says, keen to invite Atharva to Asia Plateau once he turns sixteen.

Back from Panchgani, Rohan was for the first time keeping in touch through social media and telephone calls with friends living across India. He travelled to Indore to meet one of them, then to Delhi. The workshop also gave him his first brush with entrepreneurship, a woman who had quit her job with a multinational to start her own venture. 'Until then, the only outings we ever had were to our grandmother's village in Karjat for a few days every summer, or to Belgaum to worship our family deity. This was the first time I ever travelled northwards—everything was so different.' Food, an easy thing for teens to gather around, became more than a necessary routine. 'Earlier all I wanted was that food should be nonvegetarian, but travelling helped me discover different cuisines, and really understand food as an aspect of our culture.' He explored every inch of Indore's Sarafa Bazaar, apart from street cuisines in Nagpur, Nashik, Delhi and Pune. He went trekking to Visapur fort recently, and hopes to soon get himself a GoPro camera and just 'set off alone'.

Rohan is now also dabbling in some network marketing, is looking for an internship simultaneously, and is contemplating studying law. He is an avid nature lover and animal lover, left heartbroken when his hamster died and now best friends with Dexter, an eighteen-month-old German Rottweiler owned by a friend. 'I was walking Dexter when he was still only six months old and he swallowed a large fruit that had fallen from a tree. He was choking on it and I froze for a few seconds, doubly nervous because he belongs to someone else. Anyway, I decided I had to do the best I could, so I pulled open his mouth wide and stuck my hand in and yanked the fruit out. My hand went down all the way to his throat. If he'd decided to bite, I'd have likely lost the hand,' he says, still wide-eyed at the memory. Among his heroes now are people who have it in them to show kindness to animals, 'and to all beings that cannot speak for themselves'.

Dad taught him to never lose sight of his dreams, he says, and those dreams have now stretched wide, and far, to include everything from a double-braided beard and tattoos like Jack Sparrow, once Shruti can be convinced about this, a Ducati or a BMW S1000RR superbike, a Jaguar car, skydiving in Dubai or Spain where Hrithik Roshan did it, scuba diving in Norway, in crystal-clear waters surrounded by hills. There are some real and immediate plans too, a car for mummy once he can save some money. 'It would be a dream come true if I can be settled while I am in my thirties, having earned enough money, and then go travelling alone.'

Shruti smiles indulgently every time the boys talk about cars and bikes and dream holidays to locations she knows nothing about. 'If they work for it and they are able to afford it, that's great. But I also want them to remain rooted to our realities, they should have an understanding of our struggles,' she says. It was only in late 2013, when Bollywood actor Farooque Shaikh died, that the Kambles were told he had been an anonymous benefactor for Rohan and Atharva since Rajan's death. They were filled with gratitude upon finding out. Shaikh had extended a helping hand after reading about the family in a 2008 report in *The Indian Express*, and Shruti continues to treat journalists with kindness and warmth.

Both sons are now taller than she is, and twelve-year-old Atharva has outpaced Rohan. Atharva has begun to hang out with friends in the locality they live in, leaving Shruti often alone at home. She and Rajan had a love marriage, one that defied caste and family. Having completed a nursing degree, Shruti was working at Bhatia Hospital after a brief internship at a Kalyan public hospital when she met Rajan, who had come to visit somebody else there. A very brief courtship later, the two decided to marry. That was in 1996, the kids arrived soon after and Shruti didn't have occasion to consider resuming her career, until recently. A couple of years ago, she began to feel an acute emptiness, a sort of too-early preparation for when Rohan and Atharva will invariably fly the coop. 'I felt I was stagnating, and wanted to do something useful,' she says.

She thought then that perhaps nursing was her calling—the idea of helping others in pain attracted her. But she also loves cooking, and her modaks, karanjis and shankar paale are a hot favourite in her housing society. 'I've now begun to accept orders to cater for small events, sometimes I manage on my own and sometimes I do it along with a friend, depending on the number of people we're catering for,' she says. She hopes she will be able to gradually build it into a small home business.

Rohan's newfound focus and ambition are a huge source of hope. 'Nobody ever expects that you will suddenly become a single mother to two boys, so naturally one is absolutely unprepared,' she says. Some years ago, she decided to invest much of the ex gratia sum she received after Rajan's death in a little house in their locality, one that fetches her a small monthly rent. That two sons will have a home each in the future was also part of her reasoning. A little buoyed now by the promise that Rohan has begun to show, and her own attempts at establishing a source of income for herself, Shruti has recently invested in a flat in

Karjat, in her native village. She has taken a loan, a brave step. 'It will keep me on my toes, it's better to keep working than to sit at home alone and allow memories and grief to cast their shadow over my everyday life,' she reasons. 'And anyway, Rohan has said he will help pay the EMIs once he begins to earn.'

Over the years, Shruti has made sure Rohan and Atharva know just how brave Rajan was. They are able to immediately recollect the name of the doctor who used hotel linen to try and stop the blood that night, the other guests who called and thanked her profusely for Rajan's selflessness in the face of terror, his conversation on the phone that night saying the call of duty was his first love, and that last phone call after the attack had begun when he whispered to her that he was all right. Atharva too has now stopped asking about his father, slowly comprehending what exactly happened.

The brothers engage in mock fights, and complain about each other to Shruti incessantly, but they're really inseparable, all three of them. Atharva has picked up many of Rohan's traits, is an ace at video games and loves the fish dada has brought for the new aquarium-tank. He wants a dog too, just like dada. Rohan corrects him—he wants two dogs, a Doberman and a Rottweiler. 'Jack and Daniels,' he winks.

Epilogue

It goes back further than 26 November 2008. To be precise, for some of us at *The Indian Express*, this journey began about a week after a series of bomb explosions ripped open Mumbai's lifeline, my lifeline, the suburban train network, leaving 187 people dead in July 2006. Convinced that these 187 Mumbaikers' lives were more important than another statistic, we set out to locate their families and ask how they had lived. Terror had mockingly set these families' trajectories awry, but these 187 had lived, loved, sung, studied, worked, earned, hoped, cried and prayed. And a few of us were tasked with telling their stories. But as the weeks wore on, many of the bereaved whom we were visiting couldn't comprehend why we wanted to scratch at still-healing scabs. And then there were the incomplete and incorrect addresses. Twice, I requested the editors to end the series; we had made our point, I imagined, in offering our readers a glimpse into the simple lives of those who had died, people who were anything but unremarkable to their loved ones.

It is always an unpleasant assignment to speak to the grieving. Certainly, some reporters are naturally more adept than others at holding a just-widowed wife's hand, offering a few empty but reassuring phrases, making surreptitious notes. I have felt only terror at others' grief, ridiculously out of my depths every time I poked around awkwardly at what are intensely private stories. Did he have a favourite Bollywood song? Did the two of you ever watch the Mumbai monsoon together from this porch? What made your dad especially angry? Do you have photographs of that holiday? Tell me what you said in that first love letter? Each time, the answer came gently, offered gingerly as if to a pensieve where other memories eddied around. We dragged those alien memories to our office workstations and then to dinner and then home, our poise not quite there any more.

Eventually we pressed on, and '187 Mumbai Life Stories' were published, one every day until almost mid-January of 2007. And, however, inadequately captured and told, these stories, and most of them are accounts shared by grieving women and children, collectively forced us to see and appreciate human resilience triumphing silently. In the months since the bombings, one teenager had started college, a mother had earned her first salary. Some women, having met at a tribunal hearing cases for payment of compensation, had begun to stay in touch with one another—a survivors' meet-up of sorts. The writers and readers of those stories both perceived life inching ahead right past that once insurmountable grief, lending meaning to the survivors' struggles seen over a period of time. They were just accounts, survivors' stories, and they were all we had to glean meaning, patterns and a connectedness in disparate narratives, and in their ability to do that they were uniquely powerful.

On the night of 26 November 2008, I was peering into my computer screen on the second floor of Express Towers, when barely a couple of hundred metres away two terrorists rushed into the Oberoi Hotel, firing their AK-47s. I was still wondering what had caused what I'd assumed to be a wedding procession's fireworks to end as abruptly as they'd begun when the phone rang; two men with automatic weapons had let loose a crazy spray of gunfire inside Leopold Cafe, a couple of kilometres away. We knew within minutes that it was more than a gang-war—coordinated attacks by gunmen at multiple locations, including one just across our office building. A long siege of multiple locations in South Mumbai was beginning. We stayed at our workstations that night, one explosion in the hotel across the road sending a tremor down our building, the frequent rat-tat-tat of automatic gunfire sounding too proximate in the silence of the newsroom. We made calls to check on colleagues who were on the field at various sites that were under attack.

Over the next few days, our reporters delivered striking investigative accounts of everything that had gone wrong—protocols for preparedness ignored, intelligence inputs disregarded, coastal policing absent. But there were also heart-wrenching stories of those whose daily lives would reverberate for many years with the impact of the attacks. There was Baby Sheetal, the youngest survivor at a few months, separated for agonizing hours from her mother Sunita who was herself barely out of her teens. Sheetal had lost her father at the train station, Sunita, her entire life as she knew it. Momina Khatun was four months pregnant, her husband Mohammed Umar Shaikh dead when a taxi he was driving exploded in Vile Parle. She had three older boys and one more on the way, and no means of subsistence. For the families of the 166 who died, the devastation was total, irrevocable.

The subsequent years took me to other scenes of loss. I met dozens of widows in drought-hit Marathwada, families of youngsters killed in senseless acts of caste violence. Many of them spoke of the shock at the suddenness of their loss. Everything had seemed just fine—until it wasn't. In *The Year of Magical Thinking*, Joan Didion writes of how the thoughts and memories of the grieving inevitably gravitate towards those moments before the unthinkable occurred, mundane and everyday chores being completed when suddenly everything changed. It was exactly what I heard in Marathwada, also what I'd heard from the families of those killed on board the suburban trains, and what I'd heard from families of those killed in the 26/11 attacks.

All things are indeed connected, and this was evidence. I continued to stay in touch with a few families I met in 2006, and many more I had met in 2008. Alone at home, I celebrated with a single malt when I found out that Baby

Sheetal's mother Sunita had found employment with the Railways. Another drink when, in 2016, a colleague found out she had remarried. On more than one occasion, I found that a survivor had reached out to another, a new story was beginning.

The day after Ajmal Kasab was hanged, I didn't call any of the 2008 survivors. Instead, I listened as Meeta Shah, who lost her husband Tushit in the train explosions of 2006, spoke eloquently over the phone about what closure and justice really meant, what forgiveness entailed, and where the death penalty sat wedged amid these. I was taking notes, but it wasn't for anything I would write. I just wanted to talk to her that night because her story resonated at that moment.

I had seen a congruence in dissimilar narratives earlier, and now with the passage of years I was seeing an assimilation of different stories all pointing to one thing. That grief does not pass, but people grow in strength and courage, those left behind adapt, deepen their resolve and give terror its only lasting answer—they survive, they dig out unknown reserves of resilience and nerve. If the suddenness and senselessness of their loss was the terrorist's way of mocking their lives, their continued harmonious existence with people of all faiths had the last word. Some went on to question the system and demand better preparedness. Others made it their life's mission to pay homage to a martyr. Women turned unexpectedly into breadwinners.

Sarlaben Parekh, now eighty-five, lost her only son and daughter-in-law on 26/11, but took on the Maharashtra government with a civil suit seeking better surveillance systems. Major Sandeep Unnikrishnan would have turned forty-one this year, and on his birthday his parents K. Unnikrishnan and Dhanalakshmi sent out greeting cards from their Bangalore home to a few thousand people they have met over the decade. 'Salute to you on your forty-first,' the card said, another little nudge in the couple's continuing efforts to make sure the country values his martyrdom. Back in Mumbai, Govind Singh Kathayat welcomed the birth of his little boy in February 2018, his second child. Diagnosed with schizophrenia after the attacks, he has finally put a broken marriage behind him and made a fresh start. Rohan Kamble, nineteen, who lost his father, a maintenance department staffer at the Taj, has begun to nurture dreams of entrepreneurship and travels across the world.

If, for a species that seeks out meaning, stories help find our place within the wider world, these accounts over ten years are an affirmation that there is meaning and inter-connectedness in the human existence despite the general bleakness of everything. And because anniversaries can be useful punctuations in time for us in the news industry, providing context and a sense of progress made amid headlines and news events rushing ahead, the tenth anniversary of the 26/11 attacks is an ideal time to remember these stories. They are reminders of that incredible bright light of oneness with the other.

Kavitha Iyer